The Institute of Chartered Financial Analysts
Continuing Education Series

Equity Markets and Valuation Methods

San Francisco, California
September 21–22, 1987

Paul H. Aron
Preston W. Estep
H. Russell Fogler
Robert L. Hagin
Bruce I. Jacobs
Dean LeBaron, CFA
Kenneth N. Levy, CFA
Michael L. McCowin, CFA

Barr Rosenberg
Gary G. Schlarbaum, CFA
William F. Sharpe
Jeffrey L. Skelton
Eric H. Sorensen
Meir Statman
Wayne H. Wagner

Edited by
Katrina F. Sherrerd

Susan S. Brennan, *Production Editor*

Sponsored by
The Institute of Chartered
Financial Analysts

Additional copies of this publication may be ordered from

Professional Book Distributors, Inc.
P.O. Box 100120
Roswell, GA 30077
1–800–848–0773

ISBN 0–935015–05–1

Printed in the United States of America

Contents

Foreword

The recent developments in the equity securities markets have caused many investors to pause and rethink their equity investment strategies. Many question the efficiency of the market, or the ability of the market to perform its role. Because of the dramatic changes in the investment industry, the timing of the ICFA-sponsored seminar *Equity Markets and Valuation Methods* was excellent. The seminar, held on September 21–22, 1987 in San Francisco, focused on three key topic areas in the equity investment arena: market efficiency, strategies that attempt to take advantage of apparent market inefficiencies, and valuation of equity securities. The program was organized by Susan D. Martin, CFA, Assistant Vice President—Education and Programs, ICFA. These proceedings are the result of that seminar.

The speakers shared their expertise and insights on such diverse topics as efficient market theory, market cycles, investor psychology, anomalies, valuation models, program trading, and convertible securities. We wish to extend our sincere appreciation to William F. Sharpe, who acted as seminar moderator, and to the seminar speakers: Paul H. Aron, Daiwa Securities America Inc.; Preston W. Estep, New Amsterdam Partners; H. Russell Fogler, Aronson + Fogler; Robert L. Hagin, Miller, Anderson & Sherrerd; Bruce I. Jacobs, Jacobs Levy Equity Management; Dean LeBaron, CFA, Batterymarch Financial Management; Kenneth N. Levy, CFA, Jacobs Levy Equity Management; Michael L. McCowin, CFA, Harris Trust and Savings Bank; Barr Rosenberg, Rosenberg Institutional Equity Management; Gary G. Schlarbaum, CFA, Miller, Anderson & Sherrerd; Jeffrey L. Skelton, Wells Fargo Investment Advisors; Eric H. Sorensen, Salomon Brothers Inc; Meir Statman, Leavey School of Business Administration, Santa Clara University; and Wayne H. Wagner, Plexus Group.

Special thanks are extended to Michael McCowin and Gary Schlarbaum for taking the time to comment on these proceedings prior to publication.

Darwin M. Bayston, CFA
Vice President
Education and Research

Biographies of Speakers

Paul H. Aron is Vice Chairman of Daiwa Securities America Inc., where his responsibilities include advising on international investment and corporate finance as well as research and marketing. Prior to joining Daiwa Securities, Mr. Aron was associated with the College Retirement Equities Fund and the Dreyfus Fund. He acts as a consultant to numerous agencies and companies, and has contributed articles to such publications as the *Financial Analysts Journal* and the *Wall Street Transcript*. Mr. Aron holds an M.A. from Columbia University.

Preston W. Estep is General Partner of New Amsterdam Partners. Prior to cofounding the firm, he was Director of Strategy Systems at Salomon Brothers and Director of Applied Investment Theory at Kidder Peabody. Mr. Estep has written articles for the *Financial Analysts Journal*, the *Journal of Portfolio Management*, and the *New York Times*, as well as other publications. He is on the Editorial Board of the *Journal of Portfolio Management*. Mr. Estep has been a speaker at the Institute for Quantitative Research in Finance, the Institute of Chartered Financial Analysts, the Wharton Economics seminar, and numerous other professional organizations.

H. Russell Fogler, Ph.D. is a Partner of Aronson + Fogler. Previously, he was a Professor of Management Science at the University of Florida and an academic consultant to the Frank Russell Company. Dr. Fogler has written over 25 articles as well as several books, and authored a chapter of the ICFA-sponsored text, *Quantitative Methods for Financial Analysis*. He is on the editorial board of the *Journal of Portfolio Management*. Dr. Fogler holds an M.B.A. from the University of Michigan and a Ph.D. from Columbia University.

Robert L. Hagin, Ph.D. is a Partner and Co-Director of Quantitative Research/Portfolio Management at Miller, Anderson & Sherrerd. Previously, he was Director of Quantitative Analysis at Kidder, Peabody & Co., and had founded his own firm, Hagin Capital Management. Dr. Hagin was also an Assistant Professor at the University of Pennsylvania's Wharton School of Finance. He is author of several books on investing, and has served as an Associate Editor of the *Journal of Portfolio Management*. He is a member of the Institute for Quantitative Research in Finance. Dr. Hagin holds a B.S., an M.S., and a Ph.D. from the University of California.

Bruce I. Jacobs, Ph.D. is a Principal of Jacobs Levy Equity Management. Previously, he was Vice President of the Prudential Insurance Company of America, and was Senior Managing Director of a quantitative equity management affiliate as well as Managing Director of Prudential's Pension Asset Management Group. Dr. Jacobs has served on the faculty of the Wharton School. He contributes to investment journals and is a frequent conference speaker. Dr. Jacobs holds a B.A. and an M.S. from Columbia University, an M.S.I.A. from Carnegie-Mellon University, and a Ph.D. from the Wharton School, University of Pennsylvania.

Dean LeBaron, CFA is President of Batterymarch Financial Management. Prior to his affiliation with Batterymarch, he was Vice President and Fund Manager of the Keystone Custodian Growth Fund. Mr. LeBaron is author of *The Ins and Outs of Institutional Investing*, and has written articles on investment policy and management issues for professional journals. He has served as Chairman of the SEC Advisory Committee on Tender Activities/Tender Offers. He holds an A.B. and an M.B.A. from Harvard, where he was a Baker Scholar.

Kenneth N. Levy, CFA is a Principal of Jacobs Levy Equity Management. Previously, he was Managing Director of an affiliate of the Prudential Asset Management Company. Earlier, he was responsible for quantitative research for Prudential Equity Management Associates. Mr. Levy has authored articles and spoken at conferences on a variety of investment topics. He holds a B.A. from Cornell University, and an M.B.A. and M.A. from the Wharton School, University of Pennsylvania.

Michael L. McCowin, CFA is Vice President in the Fixed Income Management Section of the Institutional Investment Management Group at Harris Trust & Savings Bank. Mr. McCowin manages the group's Convertible Securities Section and is portfolio manager for the Harris Convertible Fund. Previously, he was Vice President and Administrator of the Investment Advisory Services Division at Harris Bank. Mr. McCowin is President of the Investment Analysts Society of Chicago, and Chairman of the Council of Examiners of the Institute of Chartered Financial Analysts. He holds a B.S. from the Illinois Institute of Technology, and has attended the M.B.A. program at the University of Chicago.

Barr Rosenberg, Ph.D. is Managing Partner of Rosenberg Institutional Equity Management, which he organized in 1984. Previously, he was a Professor in the School of Business Administration, University of California at Berkeley, where he specialized in finance and econometrics. Dr. Rosenberg was a founder and first director of the Berkeley Program in Finance. He also founded BARRA, a consulting firm in modern investment technology. Dr. Rosenberg holds an A.B. from the University of California, an M.Sc. (Econ.) from the London School of Economics, and a Ph.D. from Harvard University.

Gary G. Schlarbaum, Ph.D., CFA is Co-Director of Quantitative Research/Portfolio Management at Miller, Anderson & Sherrerd. Prior to joining the firm, he was Vice President of the Asset Allocation Division of First Chicago Investment Advisors. Dr. Schlarbaum also has served as a Professor at the Krannert Graduate School of Management, Purdue University. He has authored many articles in financial journals, and was an Associate Editor of the *Journal of Financial and Quantitative Analysis* and *Financial Review*. Dr. Schlarbaum is Chairman of the Candidate Curriculum Committee of the Institute of Chartered Financial Analysts. He holds a B.A. from Coe College and a Ph.D. from the University of Pennsylvania.

William F. Sharpe, Ph.D. is President of Sharpe-Russell Research, Inc. and Timken Professor of Finance at the Stanford University Graduate School of Business. Dr. Sharpe teaches investments, theory of finance, portfolio theory, financial aspects of pension funds, and microeconomics, and has written numerous books and articles on these subjects. He is widely known for the development of the Capital Asset Pricing Model (CAPM) used so extensively in financial analysis. He is author and developer of Asset Allocation Tools, an asset portfolio optimization program. Dr. Sharpe is a member of the Council on Education and Research at the Institute of Chartered Financial Analysts. He holds an A.B., an M.A., and a Ph.D. from the University of California.

Jeffrey L. Skelton, Ph.D. is Executive Vice President and Manager of the Business and Product Development Group at Wells Fargo Investment Advisors, responsible for client relations, marketing support, and product development. Prior to joining Wells Fargo, Dr. Skelton was an Assistant Professor of Finance at the Unversity of California, Berkeley, and also served as a consultant to various firms, including Barr Rosenberg Associates and Security National Bank. Dr. Skelton has contributed articles to professional publications such as the *Journal of Financial Economics* and the *Journal of Finance*. He holds an M.B.A. and a Ph.D. from the University of Chicago.

Eric H. Sorensen, Ph.D. is Vice President and Senior Quantitative Analyst at Salomon Brothers Inc., where he leads a team in the creation of quantitative applications for equity strategy. Previously, Dr. Sorensen was Head of the Department of Finance and Real Estate at the University of Arizona. He has published over 30 articles on investments and financial markets in academic and professional journals, and is an Associate Editor of the *Journal of Portfolio Management*. Dr. Sorensen holds a Ph.D. from the University of Oregon.

Meir Statman, Ph.D. is Associate Professor of Finance at the Leavey School of Business, Santa Clara University. He is involved in researching the application of knowledge from psychology to financial decisions; one of his current research projects is supported by the National Science Foundation. Dr. Statman is a member of the Advisory Board of the *Journal of Portfolio Management* and an Associate Editor of *Financial Management*. He holds a B.A. and an M.B.A. from the Hebrew University of Jerusalem, and a Ph.D. from Columbia University.

Wayne H. Wagner is Partner and Chief Investment Officer of Plexus Group. Previously, he held the same position with Wilshire Associates, and has also served as Assistant Vice President at Wells Fargo Bank. Mr. Wagner has authored many articles and given numerous speeches on a variety of investment topics. He holds a Bachelor's degree from the University of Wisconsin and an M.S. from Stanford University.

Overview of the Seminar

The presentations made at this seminar addressed the concept of market efficiency. Every investment professional must consider carefully the meaning of this term, as Bill Sharpe points out in the introduction to these proceedings.

Like the stock market itself, our perception of efficient markets is constantly evolving. Prior to 1960, researchers investigated whether prices followed a random walk. By 1970, most researchers agreed that markets were efficient. By the 1980s, however, researchers were again searching for patterns in security returns. Efficient market research had come full circle. Gary Schlarbaum's presentation traces this evolution in our way of thinking about market efficiency.

The concept of efficient markets is central to any discussion of equity markets. At the same time, investment professionals are developing investment strategies that attempt to take advantage of apparent market inefficiencies, and are perfecting techniques to index the market. Both of these approaches are discussed in this publication.

Equity markets have undergone many changes in recent years, including the development of sophisticated computer-based trading strategies, increased emphasis on quantitative techniques, derivative securities, portfolio insurance, and many other investment products. These developments have influenced not only investment strategies, but also valuation methods. Russ Fogler and Tony Estep present valuation methods for equity securities; Mike McCowin illustrates a valuation method for convertible securities. These presentations also discuss the influence of efficient market theories on valuation.

Equity markets have entered a new era, according to Dean LeBaron. The role of the equity manager is being redefined by rapid changes in technology, globalization of securities markets, and a renewed focus on individual security values. In this new environment, the importance of having a strong investment philosophy cannot be overstated. The presentations that appear in these proceedings will provide the reader with valuable new insights on equity markets and valuation methods.

MARKET EFFICIENCY

The efficient market hypothesis has been at the center of investment theory for decades. In the program's opening session, Gary Schlarbaum explores the status of the efficient market hypothesis in today's financial environment. He begins with a definition of an efficient market, and discusses conditions that may lead to an inefficient market. He focuses on two definitions of an efficient market: first, that prices equal market value in an efficient market, and second, that prices fully reflect available information in an efficient market.

Schlarbaum points out that the view of the efficient market hypothesis is an evolving one. The thinking on efficient markets may be divided into four distinct periods: 1900–1959, the 1960s, the 1970s, and the 1980s. Schlarbaum reviews the literature and discusses the major research questions addressed in each period.

The efficient market literature really begins with the development of the random walk hypothesis, which was established in the literature between 1900 and 1959. In the 1960s, researchers began to test this theory by exploring such topics as the serial correlation of security returns, the existence of profitable trading systems relying only on past prices, the nature of the distribution of returns, market reaction to public announcements, and the ability of professional investors to provide superior performance. Researchers of the 1970s questioned whether profitable selection rules existed which relied solely on public information, and whether insiders earned excess positive returns. In the 1980s, research has turned to the investigation of exploitable patterns in returns, and the fluctuation of security prices. Schlarbaum discusses the literature that addressed these questions and provides insightful commentary on the research presented.

ENGINEERED INVESTMENT STRATEGIES: PROBLEMS AND SOLUTIONS

Rapid technological advances have changed the investment industry; the use of quantitative analysis has expanded as a result of the new techology and the increased availability of data. These changes have given rise to what Robert Hagin calls engineered investment strategies.

Hagin defines an engineered investment strategy as having at least three characteristics: (1) that the strategy is based on theory; (2) that there is an explicit or quantified statement of the strategy; and (3) that there is a precise determination of how the strategy would have worked in the past. He discusses engineered investment strategies in general, and identifies some potential problems involved in using these strategies. These problems include insufficient rationale for why an engineered strategy should work; blind assumptions; data mining; the accuracy of available historical data; the appropriateness of linear models in a nonlinear world; and the selection of a "reference" portfolio against which to measure the performance of an engineered strategy.

To resolve these problems, Hagin constructed a database without survivor bias, using Compustat data that included companies no longer in existence, and built a program that allows the user to test historical returns associated with any combination of factors and categories. Hagin provides an explanation of how the program works.

MARKET CYCLES IN THE VALUATION OF EQUITY MARKET SECTORS

This session explores the concept of market cycles. Peaks and troughs occur in the absolute level of the stock market and in the relative valuation of market sectors. This does not prove the existence of market cycles, according to Barr Rosenberg.

Rosenberg emphasizes that market cycles should not exist under a strict definition of market efficiency. Nevertheless, people believe that market cycles exist despite theoretical arguments to the contrary. He presents examples of behavior and circumstances that may cause one to believe there are market cycles.

Rosenberg argues that it is not enough that prices go up and down to define a market cycle; they must go up and down for a reason that is not explained by the intrinsic value of the stocks. He uses the example of marketing cycles to illustrate how market cycles might occur. A marketing cycle is caused by the naive belief that what goes up will continue to go up: Everybody sells the most popular investment ideas, which increases demand for securities in that sector, making the advisors look good because the securities continue to look good.

Liquidity is an important consideration as a reason for market cycles. Rosenberg observes that the net demand associated with the high turnover dynamic strategies first impacts liquid stocks, and then the market adjusts to reflect that. If one believes that illiquid stocks will move with the liquid ones, then it is reasonable to believe that the illiquid stocks will adjust following price movements in the liquid stocks. The same type of thinking may be used in examining the relative valuation of asset sectors. If money managers do not offset this demand, the market will be inefficient and there will be market cycles for sectors.

INVESTOR PSYCHOLOGY AND MARKET INEFFICIENCIES

Meir Statman focuses on market efficiency and inefficiency with respect to money managers. Statman questions why money managers continue to trade if they cannot beat the market, and why their clients continue to supply them with money. He suggests that there are two reasons why this occurs. First, people confuse noise and information, and trade on noise as if it were information; they believe that they have figured out the system. Statman terms this a "cognitive" reason. The second reason, which he defines as "emotional," is that people like to trade because it gives them pride.

In discussing the cognitive reasons for trading, Statman explores optical illusions—confusing randomness for patterns, for example—and such indicators as the Investors Intelligence Sentiment Index, which rates advisors as bearish or bullish. The Sentiment Index has been touted as a "contrary" indicator—one should buy when advisors are bearish, and sell when they are bullish. In reality, Statman points out, this index follows the market rather than leads it. This confusion between the variable that leads and the variable that follows is also a form of optical illusion.

The emotional reason for trading, says Statman, is pride. People experience pride when they invest in a stock and it goes up. When the stock goes down, however, people wish to decrease their feelings of loss and regret, and often do so by transferring the blame to their investment advisers. Statman believes that money managers remain in business because they play the role of scapegoat for their clients. He elaborates on this theory, discussing the actions that money managers take to reduce their own feelings of loss and regret, and how these actions may affect the market.

DISENTANGLING EQUITY RETURN REGULARITIES

The efficient market theory dominates investment research. In recent years there has been a proliferation of empirical results that represent departures from the conventional theory. This session provides an overview of the anamoly literature and investment strategies consistent with these findings.

Bruce Jacobs and Kenneth Levy begin by examining the evolution of common stock strategies and the discovery of cross-sectional and time-dependent return regularities. Recent research has revealed a web of interrelated anomalies. In disentangling these return regularities, Jacobs and Levy find evidence which is inconsistent with market efficiency.

The anomalies discussed are categorized into four groups: value-based regularities, earnings-expectations-based regularities, price-based regularities, and calendar-based regularities. Jacobs and Levy explore the relationships among these anomalies, and present methods for disentangling them. They argue that it is critical to "purify" the factors before using them to make investment decisions.

Jacobs and Levy discuss their research on anomalies, concluding that their results challenge the efficient market hypothesis, and that current asset pricing models seem deficient in explaining many of the return effects explored. Finally, they present three investment strategies that reflect their findings: the anomaly capture strategy, time-series modeling, and macroeconomic modeling.

INVESTMENT OPPORTUNITIES WITH INDEXING

This session explores opportunities to profit through indexing. Jeffery Skelton presents a history of indexing and how it may be used in the current market.

The agility and precision of passive management styles may be exploited in strategies that profit from efficient and timely moves across broad asset classes. Skelton describes three such strategies: index arbitrage, market tilting, and tactical asset allocation.

Skelton then discusses active and passive management styles, comparing them along three processes: portfolio construction, trading, and monitoring. He believes that passive managers—or indexers—have a more precisely controlled process than active managers, and that trading and monitoring in passive portfolios presents indexers with a real advantage: they can move more quickly and efficiently. Skelton outlines the ways in which indexers can spot potential value in the market using their monitoring and trading infrastructure to realize higher returns through increased efficiency.

VALUATION MODELS FOR EQUITY SECURITIES

The seventh session addresses valuation models for equity securities. In the first part of this session, Russell Fogler discusses the basis for using quantitative methods in the developmemt of security valuation models. Tony Estep follows with a discussion of a specific equity valuation model—the T-model.

Fogler addresses three broad issues relating security analysis and valuation models: whether security analysis is related to probability distributions, whether security analysis can be incorporated into dividend discount models (DDMs), and whether multifactor models will replace DDMs.

Fogler illustrates the application of quantitative methods to equity security analysis. First, he shows the relation between probability and security analysis by illustrating the positive skewness in security returns. He continues with an example of how probability analysis can be combined with fundamental security analysis to fine-tune DDM estimates. He shows how very simple quantitative techniques may be used to advantage.

Fogler cautions that probabilistic DDMs may not always be appropriate, and reviews four reasons for using factor models over probabilistic DDMs. He concludes with some comments on market efficiency. Although he believes that the market is efficient, Fogler admits that the definition of efficiency is important.

There are numerous valuation models for equity securities. Many of these models are based on regression models and complicated data-searching techniques. Preston Estep presents one—the T-model—which he believes is superior because of its simplicity.

According to Estep, security analysts seem to spend a great deal of time thinking about things other than expected return. For example, they worry about whether products are proprietary and whether the company faces foreign competition. Estep feels that the only thing the analyst should be concerned with is whether the stock will exhibit superior return. The T-model allows security analysts to use the forecasts that they generate to determine expected return, and thereby identify those with superior return potential. Examples of the T-model are provided to illustrate its use.

The T-model is an equation of return in terms of fundamentals. It is an analytical tool. Estep uses the model to analyze some of the so-called market efficiency anomalies. He illustrates the relationship between the observed behavior and the structure of the return-generating process modeled.

EQUITY DURATION

The concept of duration is being applied to equity securities. In this session, Eric Sorensen illustrates the concept of equity duration, and examines the implications of equity duration for portfolio management. He notes that the concept of equity duration is becoming increasingly important to plan sponsors.

Sorensen identifies three ways of thinking about duration. The first one is based on the original concept of duration: a measure of the time-weighted receipt of principal and interest cashflows. The second way of thinking about duration is as the derivative of the valuation formula—in this case, the dividend discount model. Finally, one may consider duration in

terms of the concept of volatility. Although each of these methods of calculating duration is legitimate, each method generates a different answer. Sorensen discusses these problems in terms of equity duration.

There are three key determinants of the relative duration between stocks: growth characteristics, discount rate (which is a function of risk), and the interaction between the discount rate and growth rate assumptions. Sorensen addresses these factors as well as the differences between bond and equity duration.

Sorensen feels that there are significant problems with the dividend discount model duration calculation and offers an alternative method: examination of the total (not partial) impact of interest-rate change on the stock. This approach to equity duration is illustrated with examples from several industries.

Sorensen concludes that the idea of equity duration will continue to be of interest to investors and portfolio strategists. He believes that the need to use common factors which transcend multiple asset classes is increasing the importance of equity duration.

RELATIVE INTERNATIONAL EQUITY MARKETS: THE JAPANESE EXAMPLE

Equity markets are becoming globalized, and it is important that American investors understand what is happening outside of the United States if they are to make informed decisions. Paul Aron presents a review of many of the differences in security valuation between Japanese and U.S. financial markets in this session.

Aron notes that there has been increasing Americanization of the Japanese market; yet there are still numerous differences that must be addressed before meaningful comparisons may be made. Aron criticizes those who claim that the Japanese market is overpriced relative to the U.S. market. After adjustments to make the financial statements conform on an accounting basis, Aron notes that the price/earnings ratio for the Nikkei Dow drops from an apparent 62.9 to 33.9 times. This ratio drops to 17.2 times after adjusting for differences in capitalization rates. Based on these figures, Aron states that the Japanese market is not overvalued relative to the U.S. Dow, where the corresponding price/earnings ratio is 20.3 times.

QUEST FOR THE UNIVERSAL VALUATION MODEL

The globalization of equity markets theme is extended in this session, as Dean LeBaron explores the possibilities of a universal database and global valuation models. LeBaron believes that many of the questions raised in earlier presentations as to which factors should be built into portfolio models will be solved by examining the future from an international perspective.

LeBaron begins the quest for the universal valuation model with a review of the evolution of the U.S. securities market. He defines three distinct investment eras: the individual era, the institutional era, and the corporate era. He believes that we are now entering the corporate era, which is characterized by corporations reclaiming responsibility for the pricing of their own securities. Control is important in this era, in contrast to the institutional era, which was characterized by quantitative methods that are indifferent to individual company identity. LeBaron believes that communications technology and global markets are important in this new era.

The corporate market era requires an understanding of the economics and politics of different geographic regions. LeBaron highlights differences in the major regions of the world. He concludes that perspective is important, particularly in the transition. Investors who cling to local biases will give up profits to those who move into the new era.

PROGRAM TRADING AND MARKET EFFICIENCY

Program trading emerged in the mid-1970s, when index fund managers began experimenting with portfolio-building methods that were more efficient than trading 500 stocks one by one. Program trading is still used quite extensively by index funds, but it has turned out to be extremely useful in other applications as well. Futures markets, passive products, portfolio insurance, and various arbitrage activities may use program trading as a means of actuating the strategy. Wayne Wagner examines the use of program trading by portfolio managers.

Wagner addresses market efficiency and the influence of program trading on the efficiency of equity markets. He also discusses the perception that program trading has caused market volatility to increase; he believes that this is more of a mechanical than an economic problem. Wagner notes that program trading is expensive, and thus is not appropriate for all types of trading. Nevertheless, Wagner concludes that everyone is better off if the use of program trading increases the probability of reducing the cost of providing pension benefits.

VALUATION OF CONVERTIBLE SECURITIES

In the final session, Michael McCowin highlights the nature of the convertible market, and the investment opportunities it presents. He argues that convertible securities are indeed a separate and very attractive asset class, and deserve to be dealt with as such. In his presentation, McCowin outlines different valuation methods and provides examples of how the market prices convertible instruments relative to theoretical values.

Convertibles are hybrid securities: part bond and part equity. There are many factors that affect the behavior of convertible prices; the price of the stock, interest-rate movements, the maturity of the underlying bond, and the conversion ratio are all important. McCowin explores how convertible securities respond to different factors, and compares these responses to stock and bond reactions. The attractive qualities of these securities arise from the fact that they do not behave exactly like either bonds or stocks. In valuing convertibles, the strategic perspective of individual investors must be considered.

Although these securities were once considered speculative, McCowin now believes that the convertible market is expanding as more corporate plan sponsors issue and invest in them.

Opening Remarks

William F. Sharpe

Several questions will be addressed in these proceedings.

1. Are markets efficient?
2. If markets are inefficient, are they more or less so than they used to be?
3. If there are inefficiencies, how may they be exploited? (Inefficiencies are also referred to as *anomalies*, or, to use an increasingly popular phrase, as "empirical regularities not yet fully understood.")
4. Are we deluding ourselves by overmining the data? (It is well known that if you torture a set of data long enough, it can be made to confess to any crime.)
5. Are these inefficiencies, once identified and exploited, likely to disappear?
6. Might some of these phenomena be better explained by psychology than financial economics?

In preparation for this assignment, I did a survey of the speakers' backgrounds. The results are clearly subject to selection bias, but should prove interesting, nonetheless. Five speakers in this program are *true practitioners*: they started their careers as practitioners and remain practitioners to this day. There is one *pure academic*: that is, he earns the bulk of his income at a university. Six speakers who are now full-time practitioners were once academics: some might term them *turncoats*. Of course, there has always been movement from faculty to industry; the novelty of current migrations is the fact that our speakers (and others like them) went voluntarily—at least so I am told. Finally, there are two (counting myself) that might best be described as *schizophrenics*: we cannot decide whether we are academics or practitioners.

Robert Merton, in his 1986 presidential address to the American Finance Association (published in the July 1987 *Journal of Finance*), made several points that are particularly germane to these proceedings. He described the field of academic finance as having experienced ". . . [an] evolution from [a] conceptual potpourri to a rigorous economic theory subjected to systematic empirical examination."

Merton also noted, (as many of us have) ". . . the conjoining of intrinsic intellectual interest with extrinsic application is a prevailing theme of research in the [field]." (I take this to mean that what we do is fun and we get paid for it as well.)

He also sounded a note of caution: "The later stages of this successful evolution have however been marked by a substantial accumulation of empirical anomalies; discoveries of theoretical inconsistencies; and a well-founded concern about the statistical power of many of the test methodologies."

Finally, he characterized the current state of affairs as a ". . . new-found ignorance in finance" (a phrase most assuredly fraught with meaning).

I would like to share another quote with you—one from a letter written to me on September 4, 1987, by a student at an eastern university. He states that in a finance class, "The professor showed that a higher beta value for a stock does not mean that the stock will have a greater expected return. My response to this was that it meant that CAPM has basically been disproved, and thus is useless. He [the professor] agreed. I then stated that if CAPM was useless, why is it still the basis of study for almost all investment analysis? His reply was, 'There is nothing better.' If there is nothing better than something that does not work, does this mean that there is nothing that works?"

In a sense, this conference was designed to address this issue.

These proceedings deal with the concept of *market efficiency*. It is important for every investment professional to think carefully about the meaning of this term. One definition holds that the market is efficient with regard to a particular set of information if revealing that information to all market participants would leave security prices unchanged. One way to assess our speakers' beliefs in market efficiency is to see how much they reveal here about their activities. Are their procedures based on the exploitation of anomalies? If so, they probably carry the seeds of their own destruction and hence need to be kept from being widely known and used. Or do their procedures rely on phenomena that may be expected to continue in the future? If so, the details may safely be revealed.

As the material to come will indicate, many questions have been answered. But, as is so often the case, many still remain to be answered.

Market Efficiency

Gary G. Schlarbaum, CFA

The two pillars of modern portfolio theory were newly—and firmly—established in 1970 when I first taught investments at Purdue University. The capital asset pricing model (CAPM) had been set forth by Bill Sharpe (1964) and others, and Gene Fama (1970) had just provided a cohesive framework and some firm conclusions about market efficiency.[1]

The two pillars are less solid in 1987. There is now a viable alternative to the capital asset pricing model—the arbitrage pricing model (APT)—which is perhaps the better of the two models. Many types of anomalies (perceived inefficiencies) have been discovered and many different strategies have been developed to capitalize on them. In this presentation, I am going to review the evolution of research related to and consensus thinking about the efficient market hypothesis.

It is first necessary to provide a definition of market efficiency. Two definitions of an efficient market are presented in Table 1. The first definition focuses on the idea that prices equal market value in an efficient market. The second definition focuses on the notion of information efficiency. In an efficient market, prices fully reflect available information.

One might ask why markets should be efficient. Some economists would argue that markets *must* be efficient. Table 2 shows three market conditions that are consistent with effi-

ciency as defined above. These assumptions may be relaxed considerably, and markets would still be efficient in an informational sense.

The related question is: What conditions lead to market inefficiency? Before reviewing the empirical literature, it would be helpful to establish a set of conditions that would result in market inefficiency. Table 2 lists two such conditions. The first condition is that there are different degrees of knowledge among investors; not all investors are fully informed. That, of course, is much more realistic than assuming that everybody knows everything. In addition, the ability to sell short is somehow limited by institutional arrangements. As a result, the prices of some securities are bid up too much; and the awkwardness of selling short precludes the market from bringing those prices back down.

One of the arguments for efficiency is that analysts make mistakes in assessing the value of securities, but because there are so many analysts, the mistakes cancel out and, on average, the valuation is correct. The point is that individual assessments are not always correct, but the price of the security is correct because analysts make offsetting mistakes. Jack Treynor (1987) suggests, however, that errors are fre-

TABLE 1. Definitions of Market Efficiency

Sharpe:	A (perfectly) efficient market is one in which every security price equals its market value at all times.
Fama:	An efficient capital market is a market that is efficient in processing information. The prices of securities observed at any time are based on "correct" evaluation of all information available at that time. In an efficient market, prices "fully reflect" available information.

Source: Sharpe, *Investments* (Englewood Cliffs, NJ: Prentice Hall, 1985) and Fama, "Efficient Capital Markets: A Review of Theory and Empirical Work," *Journal of Finance* (May 1970).

TABLE 2. Market Efficiency Conditions

Conditions Consistent with Market Efficiency:
- No transactions costs.
- All available information is costlessly available to all market participants.
- All agree on the implications of current information for the current price and distributions of future prices of each security.

Conditions Resulting in Market Inefficiency:
- All investors are not fully informed and the ability to sell short is limited by institutional arrangements.
- Investor valuation errors are not independent; i.e., tendency for investors to err in the same direction.

Source: Gary G. Schlarbaum

[1] See Reference List, pp. 101–103.

quently in the same direction and therefore not independent. There are large institutional investors and influential analysts who provide securities valuation services to investors. It is easy to see how mistakes may influence people and lead to a situation where many investors are erring in the same direction. If that is the case, there will be systematic biases away from the intrinsic value of a security.

MARKET EFFICIENCY: A REVIEW OF THE LITERATURE

It is impossible to discuss market efficiency without acknowledging the important contributions that Gene Fama has made throughout his career. His 1970 article set forth the framework for analyzing market efficiency that remains the textbook standard to this day (Fama 1970). That framework provides three basic categories of empirical tests of the efficient market hypothesis: weak-form tests, semistrong-form tests, and strong-form tests. The distinction among the three is the level of information being considered.

Early efficient market researchers focused on whether there was a strategy based only on past prices that would enable one to make unusually high profits. This is a weak-form test of market efficiency. Semistrong-form tests extend the set of information to include not only the history of past prices, but all publicly available information—for example, published reports and analysts' recommendations. In a strong-form test, the set of information includes *all* information—not only publicly available information, but privately held information as well. I will rely on Fama's classic article for my review of the literature prior to 1970. Fuller and Farrell's (1987) text contains a helpful summary of the recent work in this area.

EFFICIENT MARKET RESEARCH: 1900–1959

Research in the period from 1900 to 1959 attempted to answer the question of whether or not prices followed a random walk (see Table 3). Every review of efficient market literature references a work by Bachelier in France in 1900. This work was the first to propose the random walk model for security prices. The hypothesis is very specific: Successive price changes will be independent draws from the same distribution.

In the late 1950s, people began to make the observation that stock price changes appeared to follow a random walk. I am intrigued by what led them to that observation. My hypothesis is that technicians claimed to see patterns in stock price changes that allowed for profitable trading rules. Academics finally got interested enough to evaluate these claims.

Empirical evidence appeared to be consistent with the notion that stock prices follow a random walk. Harry Roberts (1959) addressed this question in an article published in the *Journal of Finance*. Roberts performed a simulation study to test whether he could replicate familiar stock price patterns using the assumption that prices followed a random walk. Using the Dow Jones Industrial Average, Roberts performed a series of draws and plotted the results. Figure 1 illustrates what he found. Panel (a) of this diagram depicts a series of prices generated by a random number generator. Those knowledgeable in technical patterns may recognize a head and shoulders pattern, which is one of the classic reversal patterns of interest to technicians. Panel (b) depicts the actual series for the Dow Jones Industrial Average in the year 1956. Obviously, the two lines are not the same; but the question is, if the panels were not labeled,

TABLE 3. Research Questions

Period	Question
1900-1959	Do prices follow a random walk?
1960s	Are security returns serially correlated?
	Do profitable trading systems exist which rely on past prices only?
	What is the nature of the distribution of returns?
	Does the market react quickly to public announcements?
	Are professional investors, on average, able to provide superior performance?
1970s	Does the market always respond quickly to public announcements?
	Are there profitable selection rules which rely on public information only?
	Do insiders earn excess positive returns?
1980s	Are there patterns in returns that are exploitable?
	Do security prices fluctuate too much?

Source: Gary G. Schlarbaum

FIGURE 1. Simulated and Actual Stock Price Levels

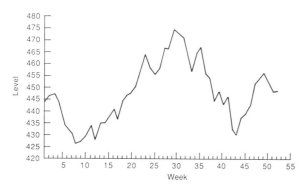

a. Simulated Market Levels for 52 weeks

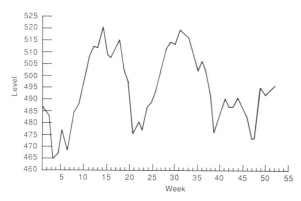

b. Friday closing levels, December 30, 1955-
December 28, 1956. Dow Jones Industrial Index

Source: Roberts, "Stock Market Patterns and Financial Analysis:
Methodological Suggestions," *Journal of Finance* (March
1959).

would you be able to identify which was the real
series and which was simulated?

EFFICIENT MARKET RESEARCH:
THE 1960s

The pace of research picked up in the 1960s (see
Table 3). A number of people were examining
the random walk hypothesis. In a 1965 paper,
Fama presented an extensive series of experiments exploring the serial correlation coefficients of changes in individual stock prices. He
looked at price changes over several time periods for the 30 Dow Jones Industrial Average
stocks. He found that daily returns exhibited a
very slight positive serial correlation, but concluded that for all practical purposes, the serial
correlation coefficient of stock returns is zero.

Once again, the evidence was found to be
consistent with the notion that the market is
efficient.

The research then moved to the next, and
perhaps more interesting question: Are there
profitable trading systems which rely only on past
prices? During this phase, researchers defined
and tested price filter rules. The hope was that
even if serial correlations were zero, there was
something more complex at work that could be
picked up with a more sophisticated test.

The literature during this period indicated
that no such systems existed. Of course, there
was a potential for bias in the published work
because there is a big incentive to hide results
that prove that money can be made with a
system—at least until the system stops working.
As an academic, I assumed that other academics
were looking for profitable strategies only until
they found one that worked; then they went out
to manage money. If they did not find one, they
published their results, and that led to tenure in
an academic institution. So it was good research
no matter how it turned out. In some sense, this
is what has happened in the 1970s and 1980s:
Many academicians have become practitioners.
A possible exception to the rule of hiding a
successful system was an article by Levy (1967)
which suggested that the relative strength rules
might have some promise.

Next, researchers tackled the question of
whether returns were normally distributed. The
answer would have an impact on most of the
empirical tests, because in most cases the tests
assumed a normal distribution. If, in fact, returns were not normally distributed, the conclusions would have to be modified. The focus was
on the fat-tailed distributions, called stable pa-
retion distributions. For the most part, the conclusion was that stock returns were probably
not normally distributed, but followed some
other kind of distribution. This conclusion created numerous problems because researchers
then had to find a substitute for the usual
analytic techniques. I am not sure that these
problems have been solved as yet. Nevertheless, by the late 1960s, the academic world was
convinced that the market was efficient in the
weak-form sense.

Researchers next turned to the question of
whether the market was efficient in the semi-
strong form: Does the market react quickly to

FIGURE 2. An Illustration of Event Time
Methodology

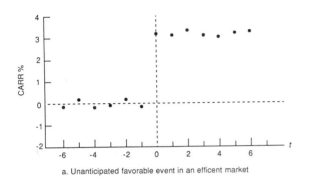

a. Unanticipated favorable event in an efficent market

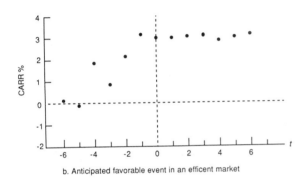

b. Anticipated favorable event in an efficent market

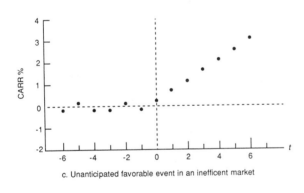

c. Unanticipated favorable event in an inefficent market

Source: Fuller and Farrell, *Modern Investment and Security Analysis*
(New York: McGraw-Hill, 1987).

public announcements? The classic work in this period is the research by Fama, Fisher, Jensen, and Roll (FFJR, 1969) on stock splits. In that article, the authors introduced the event time methodology—a technique that has been used in many subsequent studies to test the reaction of stock prices to announcements.

Figure 2 illustrates the event time methodology. FFJR focused on whether the market reacted in an efficient way to stock splits; an efficient reaction would be quick and unbiased. The research question became: Do stock prices adjust quickly, and do they go to the right level? Another way to pose the question is: Does one still have time to trade and make money after a public announcement is made, or has the price already adjusted in such a way that it is too late? FFJR's conclusion was that the market does indeed react quickly to public announcements, and it is too late to profit from a trade after a split is announced. Other kinds of announcements were quickly examined—earnings announcements, secondary offerings, and so forth. Still, the evidence supported the notion of market efficiency.

The last research question of the 1960s was a strong-form question: Are professional investors able, on average, to provide superior investment performance? This research focused on mutual funds. The logic was that if professional money managers could not provide superior returns, then the market must be efficient with respect to all kinds of information, because these managers were thought to have the most information. The answer that came back was, "No, on average they are not able to earn superior returns." Today, that conclusion might seem obvious, because "they" are everybody. Perhaps the answer was not as obvious then; institutions were becoming important, but they were still much less important in the 1960s than they are now. Perhaps a better question would have been: Can we identify any investors who have put together a consistent record? And, on the basis of that consistent record, can we conclude that this person was a skillful investor? That answer might also have come back "no." That brings us to the end of the 1960s, and everything seemed clear: Markets were efficient. They were efficient at the weak-form, the semi-strong-form, and the strong-form levels.

EFFICIENT MARKET RESEARCH: THE 1970s

During the 1970s, there was a major change in the direction of market efficiency research. Suddenly everything that was so well established— the twin hypotheses of the CAPM and market efficiency—looked a lot less firm.

The first question posed in this period was: Does the market always respond quickly to public announcements? Several studies were published that shed doubt on that conclusion. Jaffe (1974) studied whether insiders make abnormal profits using their information set, and concluded that they do. He went on to test whether information in the Official Summary, based on what insiders are doing, may be used to make above-average profits. He concluded that it was possible. This made a small dent in the armor of the efficient market theory—at the semistrong-form level at least.

Latané and all of his associates and students, many of whom are very well known in their own right today, studied whether the market responded efficiently to the announcement of quarterly earnings. His tests used Standardized Unexpected Earnings (SUEs). These studies attempted to determine how the market responded to differences between expected and actual earnings. Figure 3 illustrates the results. In this study, the earnings surprises (differences between actual and expected earnings) were divided into 10 categories—or deciles. The top decile indicates the most positive earnings surprises; the bottom is the worst earnings surprises. The important thing for purposes of thinking about semistrong-form efficiency is what happens after the day of announcement. There are some rather systematic drifts. Those stocks with positive surprises drift upward; those with negative surprises drift downward. There was an adjustment before announcement, but there was also a kind of systematic adjustment afterwards.

These findings are not consistent with the notion of efficiency at the semistrong level. They indicate that there was an opportunity to create a trading system based on earnings estimates. There were also studies of reaction to listing on exchanges, which provided very puzzling results.

There is one argument in favor of market efficiency that must be addressed. Some people will say that markets are efficient no matter what evidence is uncovered, because we still do not understand asset pricing. Therefore, all tests of market efficiency are tests of a joint hypothesis. Rejection of the joint hypothesis means that either markets are inefficient *or* the asset pricing model that is being used to test market efficiency is not correct. So, if someone holds a very strong prior belief in market efficiency, it is easy to conclude the latter.

By this time, there was a growing body of evidence that was not consistent with that joint hypothesis. One watershed event of the 1970s, from an efficient markets point of view, was the publication of the anomalies issue of the *Journal of Financial Economics* (June 1978). Ten or twelve different anomalies were reported in that issue. By the late 1970s, the profession was moving away from the conclusion that the market was not efficient only at the strong-form level, toward the conclusion that it was not efficient at the semistrong form level.

The second question asked in the 1970s was: Are there profitable selection rules that rely on public information? This kind of selection rule really has a much longer history than the 1970s. An example of the selection rule which relies on public information would be a selection rule using price/earnings (P/E) ratios. There has been a long history of research into P/E ratios, some of which was done by Paul Miller and Jay

FIGURE 3. Excess Return After Firm's "Unexpected" Earnings Announcement

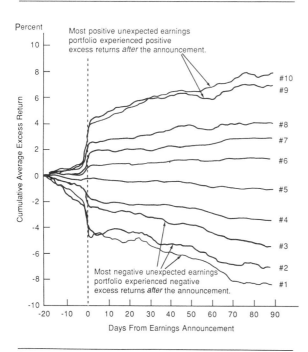

Source: Rendleman, Jones, and Latané, "Empirical Anomalies Based on Unexpected Earnings and the Importance of the Risk Adjustments," *Journal of Financial Economics* (November 1982).

FIGURE 4. S&P Returns by Day of the Week

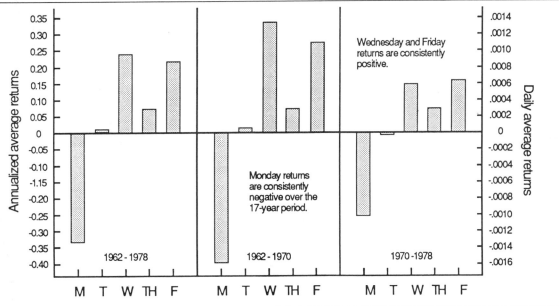

Source: Jacob and Pettit, *Investments*, (Homewood, IL: Richard D. Irwin, 1984). Calculated from Gibbons and Hess, 1981.

Sherrerd in the 1960s. Nicholson published a piece on the subject in the *Financial Analysts Journal* in the early 1960s. The finding was that low P/E stocks perform better over a market cycle.

The low P/E studies continue. The profit opportunity did not go away after the results of early P/E studies were published in the early 1960s. This body of literature was capped by the very careful work of Basu in the mid-1970s. In a piece that was published in the *Journal of Finance*, he tested the low price/earnings strategy. Basu examined a number of different asset pricing models and used a carefully selected data set. His results showed that buying low price/earnings ratio stocks was a good idea.

Fischer Black's piece on the Value-Line Survey was another important addition to the efficient market literature. It was published as a letter to the editor in the *Financial Analysts Journal* called "Yes, Virginia, There Is Hope: The Value-Line Investment Survey." Quite simply, he looked at the rankings published in the Value-Line Survey and said, "Here's something that appeared to have worked in the past." A colleage and I did a similar test on Ben Graham's selection criteria (Oppenheimer and Schlarbaum, 1981). Ben Graham, a very well known

investor, periodically published his advice to people he called defensive investors in his book *The Intelligent Investor*. So we did an experiment; we followed Graham's advice as if we had purchased *The Intelligent Investor* every time it was published. Sure enough, that advice had value. It had more value than Graham claimed, because he was quite modest in talking about his advice to the defensive investor.

Finally, the question was posed: Do insiders earn excess positive returns? The answer was yes. There were several studies on this topic, including Jaffe's work on insiders. All of them found that insiders earned positive excess returns.

EFFICIENT MARKET RESEARCH: THE 1980s

In the 1980s, efficient market research has come full circle. The first question of the decade was: Are there patterns in returns that are exploitable? We ruled out these patterns in the 1960s; now we come to the 1980s, and we have said that there is evidence not consistent with semi-strong-form efficiency. Suppose we went back to look at the weak form? One of the first papers of this phase actually appeared in 1976; it is a paper on seasonality by Rozeff and Kinney (1976). They noted that returns in January were higher than returns in other months. In the 1980s, we also discovered the size effect: Small firms tend to do better than large firms in ways that are not readily explainable by risk measures. (Yale Hirsch in the *Stock Traders Almanac* seems to have discovered this pattern long ago, as he had many of the patterns that academics discovered later.) Seasonality and size combined form the turn-of-the-year effect, a pattern which repeated itself throughout the 1960s and 1970s. Then we came to something as simple as the day-of-the-week effect, which said that Monday is not a very good day (see Figure 4). How can we explain that? Certainly it will go away because everyone is exploiting it—or so it seems.

There is a second question posed here: Do security prices fluctuate too much? Bob Schiller concludes that they do. That is clearly a source of controversy. There are others who think it is not so obvious.

So the conclusions have come full circle, from a point around 1970 when the market was believed to be totally efficient, to the point in the mid-1980s when the market appears much less efficient.

RECENT DEVELOPMENTS

Several recent developments have evolved because of research on market efficiency. The first one is the advent of index funds. Obviously, index funds have been around for awhile. The earliest reference I could find to index funds was published in the early 1970s. That seems logical, particularly given the academic perspective at the time: support for market efficiency was strong in 1970. The 1970s would be a natural time to build on the idea of index funds. Index funds have grown to account for a significant portion of the assets under management, at least in the tax-exempt realm. Approximately 30 percent of the equities under management are managed in index funds, according to *Pension and Investment Age*. That is a big percentage. And one can think of that as a result of research on market efficiency.

Going to an index fund is a natural reaction for people who conclude that markets are, in fact, efficient. Otherwise, they probably would take another approach to managing money. It is clear to me that if markets are to be efficient, it is necessary for some of the investors to be active and to be competing to earn the profits available from security mispricings. So one might expect some kind of ebb and flow in the degree of efficiency and competition. The question then arises: How have active managers performed relative to the S&P 500? They have a mixed performance to this point. Claude Rosenberg, in his recent book *Investing With the Best*, gives us a little history. The S&P 500 was formidable for managers in the early 1970s. Maybe that was part of the reason for index funds. Active managers did much better from the mid-1970s through 1982, but since then I think it has turned back the other way a little bit.

Is indexing the right answer? Is now the right time to index? I think it is dangerous to index at this particular time. The superior performance of stocks in the S&P 500 Index cannot last forever. Even now there are some strange pricing relationships.

The growth of money management firms using quantitative approaches is another important development. After finding many anomalies—different systems that work—people have decided to use those to manage money. One might argue that efficient market research was the basis for this kind of product development. The exodus from academia is persuasive evidence regarding market efficiency.

Most of the strategies used by quantitative managers are based on tests of strategies that have outperformed the market in the past. These are tests that have rejected the efficient market hypothesis, but they immediately bring up the crucial question: Will the strategies be successful in the future? I do not know.

Similarly, how long can the anomalies last? I have an interesting quote from Ben Graham in this regard: "Any approach to money making in the stock market which can be easily described and followed by a lot of people is by its terms too simple and too easy to last." Spinoza's concluding remark applies to Wall Street as well as to philosophy: "All excellent things are as difficult as they are rare." I would say if it is really easy to replicate, then its time will be relatively short. On the other hand, several of the things I have alluded to in the course of this presentation suggest that some "inefficiencies" might last for a long time; for example, the price/earnings phenomenon. I believe that it will be some time before many of these strategies disappear.

In the end, our views on market efficiency will continue to evolve over time. The efficient markets hypothesis will continue to have its advocates and its detractors. New anomalies will be discovered. New strategies will be employed. Many questions remain to be answered, and as these are answered, more will arise. This continuing interest in market efficiency is healthy for the profession, because it is here that ideas from the academe and experiences from the real world come together to create synergies that represent progress in the business of investment management.

Engineered Investment Strategies: Problems and Solutions

Robert L. Hagin

I do not expect that everyone will agree with the opinions expressed in this presentation. In fact, I hope that everyone will *not* agree with me. Clearly, if everyone agreed with me—and followed in my footsteps—the strategies that I believe can provide an important differential advantage would fail to do so.

I see little risk that this will happen, however. One of the biggest contradictions in the investment management business is that although investment managers are continuously searching for new investment ideas, most of them are slow to embrace *methodological* change. The reason is quite simple. In an "intellectual service industry" such as the investment management business, everyone needs to be different. Because we are all trying to sell our customers on the idea that we are smarter than the competition, it is very difficult to differentiate our services while embracing a competitor's methodology. To be competitive, investment managers must be different!

This means that the cornerstone of the investment management business is lack of consensus. Happily, for those of us who make a living in the business, the investment management business is alive and well. That is, of course, the same as saying that very few of us agree with one another.

Anyone who believes that there is a single theory of finance or a single approach to investment selection common to all investment managers needs only to stand on the floor of any exchange to have this belief shattered. Trading activity—the mirror of how managers differ—is carried out by people who have analyzed the same information and have reached exactly opposite conclusions. Indeed, the investment profession cannot even agree on what is an "appropriate" level of trading. Some researchers contend that there is too much trading activity; other researchers believe that the amount of trading activity is about right. Investment managers cannot even agree on what is an "appropriate" level of disagreement.

Yet, in the face of wide-ranging differences of opinion about almost every facet of the investment management business, the industry is moving in one direction: It is becoming more quantitative. This trend raises dozens of questions that, in turn, provide a new area for disagreement. Are quantitative strategies based on sufficient rationale? Are quantitative strategies based on blind assumptions that certain factors are always "good?" Are quantitative strategies the result of almost endless searches for strategies that have worked in the past (with little attention to strategies that should work in the future)?

Before turning to these questions—because I believe that understanding history can help us with the future—I would like to identify at least three reasons for the increased use of quantitative analysis: computers, people, and knowledge. For the past 30 years, successive generations of computers have provided us with capabilities that few people had ever imagined—all at lower and lower costs. And with each generation of computer hardware more people—quants—have entered the investment business. Together, the computers and the people have been able to push the knowledge base ahead at a pace that is unparalleled in the history of this industry.

Today, the tools of quantitative analysis—computers, people, and knowledge—are coming together in what I call "engineered investment strategies." I define an engineered investment strategy as having at least three characteristics: (1) The strategy is based on a sound theory—a reason why it has worked in the past and, most important, why it should work in the future; (2) There is an explicit "quantified" statement of the strategy; (3) There is a precise determination of how the strategy would have worked in the past.

I feel that the last point is the most important. Unless we know precisely how a particular investment strategy would have worked in the past, how can we *even contemplate* using it in the future?

POTENTIAL PROBLEMS WITH ENGINEERED INVESTMENT STRATEGIES

Engineered investment strategies are not without problems. In this section I identify a long list of potential problems in the design and/or implementation of quantitative investment strategies.

Insufficient Rationale: A common problem with engineered investment strategies is that there is insufficient rationale for why the strategies should have worked in the past and, most important, why they should work in the future. Suppose, for example, that I offer to present a model that has correctly forecast the direction of the S&P 400 for 19 of the past 20 years. That record—which in probability terms represents a 95 percent confidence level—should spark everyone's interest.

The model is: If the National Conference wins the Superbowl, the S&P 400 will go up in that year; if the American Conference wins, the S&P 400 will go down. As this "model" shows, it is not enough to find strategies that "work." You must start with a theory—a reason to expect the relationship to persist.

Blind Assumptions: Another problem with some engineered investment strategies is that they are based on "blind assumptions." My favorite blind assumption is that a high return on equity is always "good." (Our research shows that companies with high returns on equity, as a group, provide lower returns.) I find it amazing that in a world in which one can easily test the returns associated with any quantifiable measure, many people still make investment decisions based on blind assumptions as to what is "good" and what is "bad."

Data Mining: Another item on my list is related to the problems of insufficient rationale and blind assumptions. Imagine that you are teaching a course in statistics and ask two students in your class to toss a coin 1,000 times and report back the number of heads. One student reports 500 heads, and the other student reports 550 heads.

You might accuse the student who reported 500 heads of not really conducting the experiment. Your reasoning might be that, even though you expect 500 heads, you do not really expect exactly 500; you expect some variance around 500. You might tell the student who reported 550 heads that such deviations are expected and caution the student not to expect the same bias on the next experiment.

Financial researchers should never forget two important facts: the world is not perfect and there is very little historical information. If a researcher conducts 1,000 experiments on purely random variables, with 99 percent level of confidence, on average 10 should appear to satisfy the objective function.

What is worse, everyone scrutinizes the same data. If purely accidental relationships are there—and statisticians know they should be—they will be discovered. Thus, the publication of several papers on the same anomaly merely serves to confirm that the anomaly was there in the past, not that it will necessarily be there in the future!

In my opinion, good financial research starts with a rationale for why an investment strategy should work, it does not contain the bias that certain factors are always "good"—or always "bad"—and avoids the all-too-common problem of data mining.

Quality of Data: Computer-based historical data—the cornerstone of modern financial research—frequently suffer from problems of inaccuracy, omissions, and survivor bias. Survivor bias is the most problematic. Most computer-based data are designed for security analysts who are interested in analyzing potential investments. When studying what would have happened in the past one needs to include the companies that have disappeared as well as those still in business.

The importance of this problem is illustrated by the following story: I recently spoke with a researcher who said that he had found a very interesting model: purchasing stocks of companies that had lost money and whose stock price was less than $10. Using a database that contained only surviving companies, this researcher found what he claimed were phenomenal investments. He had forgotten, however, about the companies with stock prices below $10 that had lost money and disappeared.

There are also the problems of inaccuracy

and omissions. These problems exist with any database, and it is admittedly an enormous task to clean up such data. Because computer-based data provide the cornerstone of quantitative research, however, it is my contention that the quality of the underlying data deserves much more attention than it receives.

Look-Ahead Bias: Some engineering strategies still suffer from the problem of look-ahead bias. In its most rudimentary form, this involves using data that are not yet available. An example might be assuming that on December 31 you can calculate a P/E ratio using calendar year-end earnings.

I was at a conference recently where a participant reported he had discovered the exact mix of factors that would have provided the highest returns over a sample period. The strategy was then "tested" on the *same* sample period. As you might guess, it worked pretty well. Then came an even bigger leap of faith: The researcher introduced an investment management product into the marketplace that uses this exact mix of factors—making the rather heroic assumption that the same factors and the same weights would remain stationary in the future. Of course, they would not. (This problem can be corrected by using a hold-out sample—by specifying a model using data from one period and testing the model using data from another period.)

Multiple Factors: Returns associated with certain factors, such as size, can be very misleading unless studied in a multiple-factor context. On one hand, factors that are highly correlated—or different models that are highly correlated—pick up the same effect. Adding highly correlated factors to a model neither increases return nor lowers risk. On the other hand, sometimes factors that are not important by themselves do interesting things when combined with other factors—a much more subtle problem. Untangling these relationships presents an interesting challenge.

Possibly because untangling factors may be difficult, there is a tendency for people to think that two factors are better than one. Therefore, when two strategies work, people tend to want to combine them. This may be a waste of time (even though the marketing people seem to like it). Strategists need to remember that if the returns from seemingly different models are often highly correlated, there is little advantage in combining them.

Nonetheless, many organizations have multiple earnings models, multiple dividend-discount models, and so forth, embedded in their strategies. We need to ask whether these almost identical models are really statistically different from one another and whether anything is gained from putting such models together. Perhaps all they are doing is fooling themselves. People who are going to use multiple selection criteria *must* understand what these multiple models are doing and must have hard evidence that combining factors lowers risk and/or increases expected return.

Past versus Future: Will the future be like the past? This is the Achilles heel of empirical research. Clearly, we can never say (with complete confidence) that the future will be like the past. This does not, however, minimize the importance of studying the past. Should one use strategies that have *not* worked in the past? Absolutely not! Can one use the past as a gauge of the present? Yes! We can ask, for example, how frequently a particular event has occurred in the past.

Statistical Assumptions and Techniques: Statistical assumptions and techniques, particularly those involving the assumption of normality of investment returns, frequently raise questions about the validity of experimental results. We know, for example, that stock prices are not normally distributed. As far back as 1966 Fama wrote, "The infinite variance assumption has important implications. If variance is infinite, statistical tools such as least-squares regression that are based on the assumption of finite variance may in fact lead to very misleading answers."

We need to ask ourselves: How much of what we do is based on the assumption of normality? The answer is that researchers make two common mistakes: (1) They apply statistical tests that assume normal data (when historical prices are not normally distributed) and (2) They generate historical prices synthetically by assuming that the prices are generated by a log-normal generating process (when it is known that they do not conform to this distribution).

Linear Models: A related issue is whether researchers are being misled when they apply linear models to a nonlinear world. Both the capital asset pricing model and the arbitrage pricing theory are based on linear models. Lots of parametric statistics also use the assumption of linearity. Richard Grinold recently examined 12 BARRA factors over 168 months and found that 83 percent of the factors conformed to linear models. This means, however, that 17 percent of the factors did not conform to linear models. In this era of quantitative analysis it is extremely important to be concerned about the assumption of linearity and the structure of these models.

Laboratory to Real World: It is a *giant* step to move from a model that produces significant statistical results to developing and implementing real-world trading strategies that actually capture those significant excess returns. It is not uncommon to take a strategy with wonderful statistics and lose *all* of the value added in implementing the strategy.

Market Impact: It is especially difficult to estimate in advance the impact of one's own presence in the market. Nonetheless, reasonable assumptions as to one's impact on the market must be included as part of the analysis of any quantitative strategy. (Significant statistics are *not* enough.)

"Reference" or "Normal" Portfolios: As with any portfolio, care must be taken to select a normal or reference portfolio against which to measure performance of an engineered strategy. Consultants are very interested in this issue. If we look back, there are many periods in which equal-weighted portfolios have beaten the S&P 500 because of the size effect. Recently I read that a researcher tested 1,200 dividend-discount models and found that each model beat the S&P 500. I had fun drumming up 1,200 randomly selected equal-weighted portfolios and found that over the same period they all beat the capitalization-weighted S&P 500. The point to remember is that until a legitimate reference portfolio is constructed, we cannot say that we are deriving value from any strategy.

Measurement of Skill: A problem with any investment strategy is the time it takes to prove that a manager has skill. How long would it take to determine that a market timer who produced a net 2 percent return per year with a standard deviation of 6 percent had skill? The answer is 36 years! The techniques for parsing out skill, and what some consultants are doing in the performance measurement area, are extremely important.

HOW DOES ONE RESOLVE THESE PROBLEMS?

Our approach to solving these problems was to construct a research "laboratory" composed of:

- An extensive financial database—currently going back more than 25 years—that does not suffer from the problem of survivor bias;
- A generalized computer program that allows us to test the historical returns associated with any combination of factors and/or categories; and
- A rebalancing simulator that allows us to study the impact of changes in assumptions and trading costs

Figure 1 illustrates what one would see on a computer screen using the software that we have developed to analyze the returns associated with *any* combination of factors and/or categories. In this case, a factor is something like a P/E ratio or the expected return from a dividend-discount model. This example is somewhat arbitrary; it is meant to illustrate this research tool. The figure shows that companies with capitalizations greater than $300 million in current dollars (adjusted by the S&P 500's return); the analysis period is December 31, 1968 through December 31, 1986; the rebalancing frequency is quarterly. The P/E factor is selected (technically it is E/P and negative earnings are included) and there are five categories ordered from high to low, represented by the columns. A totally independent classification—size, defined in terms of equity capitalization—is represented on the left axis and ordered from small to large, represented by rows. For each portfolio the universe-relative annual return, that is, the return relative to the universe, is displayed.

The figure shows that the average annual universe-relative return from the high-P/E portfolios (represented by column A) was −5.3 percent over the 18-year period. The P/E factor averages increase monotonically as one moves from the high-P/E to the low-P/E quintile (the line lableled "column averages").

The row averages show that the average annual universe relative return from the small capitalization portfolios (represented by row 1) was 0.6 percent over the 18-year period. Moving down the row-average column, we see some evidence of a small-size effect; the smaller companies provided higher returns.

FIGURE 1. **Strategy Evaluation Software—An Example: Average Annual Universe Relative Returns**

P/E Quintiles- High to Low

		High A	B	C	D	Low E	Row Averages
Small→	1	-6.2	-3.8	0.5	1.3	8.0	0.6
	2	-5.0	-4.5	-0.2	3.9	8.7	1.1
Size Quintiles Small to Large	3	-5.9	-1.4	-0.8	2.0	5.2	0.1
	4	-4.2	-1.5	-4.0	2.8	6.4	-0.4
Large→	5	-3.0	-2.1	-3.6	-0.3	3.8	-1.8
Column Averages		-5.3	-2.5	-1.6	2.1	6.6	

Source: Miller, Anderson & Sherrerd

One of the things that may be done with this information is to examine the returns associated with various combinations of factors. For someone interested in the size effect in conjunction with a low-P/E strategy, column E is particularly interesting. There are statistically significant differences within Column E, showing that someone using a low-P/E strategy would have been better off buying the small companies in this universe. In fact, although the large low-P/E companies beat the universe, they did so to a much lesser degree than did the smaller companies.

It should be emphasized that the analysis of the P/E size effects in the figure is intended to illustrate one of the tools in our research "laboratory." A similar analysis may be performed on any subset of companies, over any period, for any combination of quantifiable factors. Then, as the research process unfolds, having determined that particular combinations of factors have provided excess returns, we turn to our rebalancing simulator. Using appropriate hold-out sampling procedures, we can study the impact of changes in information (what do we do, for example, when a "just qualified" P/E rank of 100 moves to a "just unqualified" rank of 101), changes in security weights, changes in rebalancing frequency, available liquidity, market impact, commissions, management fees, and expenses.

In summary, an engineered investment strategy should be structured so that it:

- Starts with a rationale for why an investment strategy should work;
- Does not contain the blind assumption that certain factors are always "good"—or always "bad";
- Avoids the all-too-common problem of data mining;
- Pays particular attention to the nature and quality of historical data;
- Relies on an experimental design that avoids the problem of look-ahead bias;
- Untangles the interactions between factors before constructing multiple-factor models;
- Measures on-going experience against expectations derived from historical studies;
- Utilizes appropriate statistical techniques (and does not overlook the fact that security prices are not normally distributed);
- Questions the assumption of linearity and the structure of the underlying models;
- Analyzes the real-world costs of implementing a strategy;
- Includes assumptions as to market impact;
- Utilizes legitimate benchmark portfolios against which to compare both historical and future performance; and,
- Parses out the sources of the excess return derived from the strategy.

Question and Answer Session

QUESTION: Why do you stop at capitalization of $300 million when the small firm effect seems to exist for much smaller companies?

HAGIN: We do not stop at $300 million—I just used that figure to illustrate a point. We have a product, a small capitalization portfolio, and that is invested in companies in the range of $50 to $300 million. But this category is not interesting if you have a lot of money. In fact, our studies showed we could manage $400 million effectively; but being very good quants, we have chosen to be conservative, and accepted only $200 million for the portfolio.

QUESTION: What percent of actively-managed portfolios is being managed quantitatively?

SCHLARBAUM: I am not sure. However, I have heard that 30 percent of the managers who are actively managing are using quantitative techniques and another two-thirds or so have some quantitative aspect as part of their process.

QUESTION: Should portfolio managers consider active management instead of indexing?

SCHLARBAUM: Active management is a good idea. The return to S&P 500 membership since 1980 has been 3.5 percent. How long can this go on? This is creating considerable valuation disparity. Consequently, one should be concerned about moving to indexing at this point.

QUESTION: Doesn't growth of indexing reflect risk aversion on the part of plan sponsors, i.e., unwillingness to underperform a given index, rather than an admission that markets are in fact efficient?

SCHLARBAUM: That could easily be the case. Another reason to index is that some pension funds are so big that it is a problem for them to consistently outperform if they manage all of the money actively. In those cases, the sponsors are not necessarily concluding that markets are totally efficient; rather they are making a con-cession to size. Indexing may reflect the internal manager's risk aversion as opposed to the sponsor organization's. The internal person charged with the responsibility of managing a fund may use indexing as a risk-averse strategy, because it avoids the situation of underperforming the index.

QUESTION: There seems to be an implicit assumption in the back tests of quantitative models that the CRSP and Compustat databases contain a complete data set, encompassing all states of financial economics. Is this assumption correct?

HAGIN: Not totally; there are data limitations. But we work with what we have. My remarks were intended to focus on the need to be aware of the biases and limitations in readily-available data sources.

QUESTION: The early studies on efficient markets were done on NYSE data. Has anybody done similar studies of OTC data, and if so, what are the results?

HAGIN: There is good OTC data starting in about 1980. But if 1973 and 1974 are not included in an analysis—and you do remember those years, the Dow and S&P 500 went down 40 percent—you are really misleading yourself. Therefore, it is hard to conclude anything from it.

QUESTION: Are the S&P 500 returns normally distributed?

HAGIN: The real expert on those data is Rex Sinquefield. He conducted an experiment that went something like this: He went to S&P 500 data and drew out two price observations and asked, "Can I determine whether this is or is not normally distributed?" No, he did not have enough. He choose a third price observation. Now, was it normal or not normal? He continued this process using a Monte Carlo simulation. At 14 observations he could reject normality. It is truly not normal. Rex is the expert on that, but by any statistical test, the S&P 500 is not normal.

QUESTION: How should small sample sizes which occur when you look at multifactor cross-classifications be handled?

HAGIN: Beware of the problem and do not let it happen. Do not look simultaneously at 42 different factors, for example.

QUESTION: Have you created a model which you find to have predictive value?

HAGIN: We have found models that worked well statistically in the past—and they were developed with appropriate hold-out sampling techniques. The models are based on theory. They have all the right underpinnings. Will these things continue to work? If they worked with certain probabilities in the past, we have theoretical reasons or rationales or hypotheses suggesting why they should continue to work.

QUESTION: Will all these techniques which seem to have worked at least in the recent past (euphoric as it may have been), perform equally well in a down market?

SCHLARBAUM: One thing is obvious, as the market goes down, index funds are going to go down with it, because index funds are an attempt to replicate the market. And we can be relatively sure that managed portfolios are going to go down as the market goes down. The question then is, How do they perform relatively? I would say that these strategies work every bit as well, relatively, in a down market as they do in an up market, and probably a little bit better in a down market than they do in an up market. That is not to say that these techniques can earn a positive rate of return if the market goes down 22 percent in 1988. (Those believing in presidential cycles, of course, would not believe that the market is going to go down 22 percent in 1988.)

Market Cycles Versus the Efficient Market

Barr Rosenberg

There is widespread belief in market cycles. In the common view, an equity market cycle bottoms out when stock prices reach a trough, and tops out when stock prices peak. Active investors also tend to believe in cycles in the relative valuation of broad equity market sectors. For example, at this moment small stocks seem to be in the lower phase of their cycle of valuation relative to large stocks: small stocks have underperformed large stocks for more than three years after previously outperforming large stocks for six years.

Peaks and troughs occur in the absolute level of the stock market, and it is equally clear that peaks and troughs occur in the relative valuations of market sectors. This does not necessarily prove the existence of market cycles, however. Random walks have no cyclical tendency towards self-reversal, and so it is not correct to refer to "market cycles" in the world of random walks. Nevertheless, random walks do produce peaks and troughs. The key question is: How does one know that the observed peaks and troughs are signs of market cycles?

To underscore this question, it is helpful to introduce a rather cynical definition of the market cycle: money managers believe that a market cycle is half over when they have recently underperformed the market, and they refuse to acknowledge that the cycle is complete until their performance has caught up.

Perhaps each of us can recognize an element of truth in this definition. When our investments perform poorly, we feel that the market is foolishly ignoring an obvious opportunity, and we are confident that when the market comes to its senses, the fall in value will be reversed. By its nature, a cycle reverses itself. Therefore, if we have performed poorly, it is comforting to think that we are halfway through a cycle; and if we do subsequently catch up, then we are convinced in retrospect that a cycle did occur. In this way, the concept of the market cycle may arise out of wishful thinking.

The concept of the market cycle also assists money managers to persuade clients to take a long-term perspective on performance. Fair evaluation of a money manager requires that the client wait at least one market cycle; when asked to define the length of the market cycle over which to be evaluated, one might answer: "Well, about two generations—or at least five years."

It is one thing to acknowledge that market cycles may be illusions; it is quite another thing to assert that there are no such cycles. My impression is that cycles in the relative valuation of equity market sectors are quite real, and that they do violate market efficiency. Unfortunately, I can offer only one short-term cycle as evidence to support this point.

A true market cycle is a sign of an inefficient market, because it implies that prices are at one time "unfairly" low, and later on are "unfairly" high. The definition of an "unfair" price is a price at which an investor may earn a superior rate of return after adjustment for risk, if he or she trades at that price.

Believers in efficient markets are understandably skeptical about the existence of market cycles. Their skepticism relies on the basic insight that stock prices do not exhibit reversals in an efficient market. Price decreases are equally likely to be followed by another decrease as by an increase. The cumulative rate of return on an asset is not likely to reverse itself—which implies that there cannot be market cycles.

To appreciate the implications of this idea, let us try a thought experiment. Suppose that there is a regular business cycle. In business cycles, earnings and dividends fluctuate. Will a business cycle give rise to a market cycle in an efficient market? No. Although stock prices will rise and fall in an efficient market along with a predictable business cycle, expected returns on stocks will not cycle; instead, they will be steady.

How is this possible? At the beginning of a boom period, a stock's price will be at a peak, in expectation of payment of substantial dividends based upon boom earnings. During the boom, the stock's price will fall as it pays out dividends. By the time the boom has ended and the trough is beginning, the stock's price will have fallen to its lowest point, because there are no prospects for dividends in the near future. Then, during the trough period, the stock's price will rise in anticipation of increased dividends during the next boom. Prices rise from a trough to a peak during the recessionary period, and then as dividends increase, prices fall from a peak to a trough during the boom period. During the boom, return comes in the form of dividend yield; during the recession, return comes in the form of capital gains. Although the price fluctuates, the return is stable. So there is a cycle in prices, but not in returns.

Of course, if the business cycle is unpredictable, then as the economy's prospects change unpredictably, the market's return will also move unpredictably to the same degree. But this pattern is unpredictable, not cyclical. In short, our natural intuition that a regular business cycle should give rise to a regular market cycle is not correct.

DEMONSTRATING A MARKET CYCLE

How might we identify a market cycle so that all would agree? An unambiguous demonstration would have to prove that (1) prices had moved to an extreme that was likely to be reversed in the future, and (2) it was possible to predict the future reversal. Then one could truthfully claim that one was halfway through a cycle.

To verify a market cycle, one needs to demonstrate predictable reversibility. One way to do this is to find investors who have always timed the market correctly. Unfortunately, among the many investors who have tried to time the market, the proportion who have achieved consistent successful performance seems to be no higher than chance would allow. This does not prove that it is impossible to time the market, but it does suggest that there are no obvious cycles which investors may reliably exploit.

Another way to verify market cycles is to find an indication that prices have fluctuated more widely than the consensus view of under-

lying value has. Historical data may be used to compare the historical trend of value in the market to the historical trend of prices. If prices fluctuate more than value, then it may be argued that the excessive swings in prices are evidence of market cycles: prices swing too far and subsequently pull back towards their underlying value.

Looking at the historical record, the market index has fluctuated far more than economy-wide dividends have. Most individuals who look at historical price and dividend fluctuations conclude that there are market cycles. Many academicians, using statistical methodology, are also persuaded that there are market cycles. Given the history of dividends over the past 100 years, it seems that investors should not have been so pessimistic as to let prices go so low, nor so optimistic as to drive prices so high.

One counterargument claims that the actual history of dividend fluctuations understates the true uncertainty that prevailed. For example, with hindsight we look back on 1933 with the knowledge that the Depression was going to end; and that Communists were not going to take over the country; but investors did not know this in 1933. Investors at that time might have legitimately feared that the United States would undergo a revolution in its economic system, but this possibility does not show up in the actual history of dividend price variability. Hence, historical dividends may not tell the whole story, because there was a probability of the whole thing falling apart, even though it did not. Nevertheless, this probability would have to have been quite high to account for the extreme in market prices, and so this counterargument is not entirely persuasive.

Earlier, I said that efficient market theorists do not believe that market cycles exist. This is not quite true. Investment returns in an efficient market may fluctuate cyclically if investors' discount rates fluctuate cyclically. The fundamental value of a stock is associated with the discounted present value of subsequent dividends. In a dividend discount model, there must be something to discount—dividends; and something to discount them by—a discount rate. The discount rate is the sum of the risk-free interest rate plus the risk premium for stocks. It is possible to explain a market trough by an increase in the risk premium for stocks, possibly due to an intense need to guarantee near-term consumption. If things are really difficult for society, the risk premium will rise, causing prices to fall. Thus, if you interviewed people in the middle of the Depression and asked them, "Why are stock prices low?" they might have answered, "Because I am hungry." It was not relevant to them that stocks were a bargain, because they were not ready to risk investing in stocks at that time.

For the market as a whole, it is not easy to understand how the risk premium could have risen high enough to account for the fall in prices in the Depression. Nevertheless, discount rate fluctuations are an interesting aspect of market cycles. In rough times, a long-term investor with an unchanged risk premium may be able to find a genuine bargain in the stock market even if the market is efficient, because the rise in other investors' discount rates permits a high expected return for stocks.

CYCLES IN THE RELATIVE VALUATION OF MARKET SECTORS

I would now like to discuss reversible cycles in the relative valuation of equity market sectors. It has been asserted that many cycles exist, including: small stocks (relative to large stocks), growth stocks (relative to high-yield stocks), high-quality stocks (relative to secondary stocks), and liquid stocks (relative to illiquid stocks).

Empirical studies show convincingly, for instance, that small stock performance has varied relative to large stock performance. To my knowledge, however, there have been no academic empirical studies that compare the relative valuation of small and large stocks. One straightforward approach would be to compare dividend series with price series to see if the fluctuation in relative value can be explained by variation in the dividend stream. Because small companies and large companies share many common features, the range of relative valuations should not be as great as it would be, for example, when comparing stocks with bonds. With the exception of liquidity—an exception which may not be justifiable—it seems reasonable that roughly the same risk premium and the same future uncertainty should apply to both large and small stocks.

Obviously, market cycles in sector valuations have important investment implications.

For example, the Dow Jones Industrial Average has lately outperformed the market as a whole as well as most money managers, partly because of the Dow's emphasis on manufacturing companies, and partly because of its emphasis on large stocks. Now, is this because of a market cycle that has peaked and is likely to reverse in the future, or is it a reversal of a past cycle (after all, the Dow underperformed for the previous decade), or is it justified by increased relative value of the Dow stocks? If the market is now at the peak of a cycle, the Dow is overpriced. One could determine if the Dow is overpriced by comparing it with other stocks on a measure of value, for example dividend yield. If the yield on the Dow stocks is substantially lower than the yield on other stocks, all other things equal, then one might say, "The Dow is now at the peak of a cycle that is going to reverse in the future." On the other hand, if the yield on Dow stocks was unusually high in the recent past, and has since fallen to more normal levels, then one might argue that Dow stock prices were too cheap, and that the recent recovery was just the reversal of an earlier cycle. And if the changes in the Dow's level have roughly paralleled changes in dividends, then one might deny the existence of any market inefficiency.

This type of research looks at the history of price/value ratios and contrasts them across sectors. The above example is fairly simplistic, because only current dividends have been selected as an index of value. Other commonly accepted measures of value are earnings, earnings forecasts, cashflow, asset value, past prices, and forecasts of long-term earnings growth or dividend growth—all of which are indications of the company's fundamental value. In fact, the use of dividends as a measure of value is suspect at present, because large companies have modified payout strategies, turning from dividend payments to stock buybacks, so that yields on large companies have fallen. Therefore, it is appealing to use a more stable indicator of value. For instance, one could use the time series of earnings for each of two sectors as the measure of value, and study the two time series of prices to determine if the relative price fluctuations were justified by the relative movements in earnings.

The recent performance of the Dow shows the relevance of this approach. Recently, Dow

Jones earnings have gone up far more than the typical company's earnings. Perhaps the Dow stocks rose in value simply because the companies finally had some earnings increases, after years of suffering from international competition. Therefore, recent events may not reflect a market cycle at all.

THE "MARKETING" CYCLE: A CAUSE OF THE MARKET CYCLE?

Are there market cycles for sectors? It is fairly obvious that there are "marketing" cycles for sectors. When a sector performs well, specialists in that sector can sell their services to naive clients based upon past total performance. Successful marketing results in inflows of funds. To the extent that specialists in a sector succeed in marketing, it is probable that there will be increased demand for the stocks in that sector. This increased demand may further enhance sector performance, and produce a feedback loop.

This rationale for a market cycle is akin to the "accelerator" which gives rise to the business cycle. Imagine that we are all growth managers and that growth stocks do well. With a gleam in our eyes, we go to prospective clients; and as they hire us, the money goes into growth stocks. Then, because of all this fresh money going into growth stocks, those stocks go up—for a time. This pattern might, to a money manager, be a natural explanation for cycles. It is possible to calculate the total value of the net inflow—that is, the value of new hires—and thus understand the importance of this market force.

The efficient market enthusiast might accept the demand cycle for stocks, created by naive clients who believe that what goes up will continue to go up. They would argue, however, that there will be a counteracting bet against this trend by knowledgeable participants in the market, "sector rotators," who recognize this unsustainable momentum and therefore sell their stocks to the newcomers, mitigating most of the excessive rise in prices.

"Net naive demand" for the stocks of a sector is one of the many possible causes of a cycle in the sector's valuation. The cycle will not occur, however, if there is offsetting "net wise supply." In this terminology, a "net offset" means that the net demand is offset by an accommodating net supply, and "wise" means that the accommodative trade is done in recognition of the fair value of the two sectors, and motivated by the superior expected return resulting from the trade.

The debate among knowledgeable investors regarding the importance of market cycles often comes down to a difference of opinion about the amount of superior return that is required to evince enough wise supply to offset the naive demand. Common sense suggests that the larger the naive demand, the greater will be the necessary price move required to induce wise investors to satisfy it, and thus the larger the market cycle. To frame a specific question, how large a price increase is required before wise investors are ready to sell 10 percent of the stocks in a sector to naive investors? If the necessary price move is 25 percent, then we have a big cycle. If the necessary price move is 1 percent, then the cycle essentially vanishes. Obviously, the answer depends upon the proportion of the investors in the sector who are "wise," as well as upon the readiness of those investors to expose themselves to the risk of the sector's return.

RECENT UNDERPERFORMANCE OF SMALL SECONDARY STOCKS

The small stock phenomenon has been in many people's minds lately, because small capitalization stocks, after having on average outperformed the S&P 500 for a long while, have recently underperformed. This is very discouraging for those investing in the wrong sector. On the other hand, small stocks did very well from 1977 through 1982. Why did the small stock sector do so well in those years, and why has it underperformed lately? Can this be explained by changing relative demand, possibly associated with a market cycle, or by a relative change in the expected profitability of small companies, as would be the explanation in an efficient market?

There was increased demand for small stocks during the 1970s. The growth of active and passive managers specializing in small stocks in the 1970s may be one explanation. At that time, there was an emerging belief that the market was more efficient for liquid stocks than for secondary stocks. Perhaps investors bought small secondary stocks in pursuit of special opportunities, and average small stock prices went up significantly as a result. There may be other explanations of which I am unaware.

It is interesting that during the period that the small stocks were going up, there were not many academic studies, so the explanation for the rise is not likely to be found in academic research. On the other hand, the recent fall, just after a spate of academic publicity, may be sheer contrariness on the part of the market!

Of course, one can shed light on whether this rise may have been part of a cycle by tracking the dividend or earnings flows of small companies to see whether, when their prices were rising, their earnings and dividends were also rising proportionally. If they were, then there is no need to search further for an explanation of the price rise.

It might be useful to refer again to the biases of investment specialists. Small stock managers tend to believe that small stocks were undervalued at the beginning of this price rise and fairly valued at the end; large stock managers argue that small stocks were fairly valued at the beginning and overvalued at the end. Perhaps if I emphasize such biases, you will be able to take an unbiased view of such questions.

Small stocks have lagged recently. Can we explain the performance in terms of falling demand for small stocks? Alternatively, can we explain the fall in terms of increased demand for large stocks? I see three factors that may have led to increased demand for large, well-known, liquid stocks, and so might have given rise to the beginning of a cycle: the growth of S&P 500 index funds, net investment by foreign investors, and net purchases of liquid securities by portfolio insurers in a rising market.

It is possible to point the finger at index fund investors, because passive funds usually index the S&P 500 instead of the market as a whole. Therefore, most of the flow into equity index funds has gone into the S&P 500, requiring disposal of previous holdings of the 30 percent of the market outside of the S&P 500. Data on the flow of money into index funds is generally available, and the flow has been large. Using that data, one can consider whether the flow was large enough to cause a market cycle, in view of the readiness of active money managers to exchange S&P 500 stocks for non-S&P 500 stocks at a premium return. How much overvaluation of the S&P 500 would provide

sufficient profit for the accommodating traders? Perhaps the size of the flow overwhelmed the capacity of sector rotators, so that a large relative price change was required to accommodate this volume.

Another explanation for growing relative demand for large stocks is net foreign investment in the U.S. market. Most foreign investment houses follow a relatively short list of U.S. stocks, and rarely invest outside of their followed list. It is easy to confirm that foreign investors' followed lists are made up of the larger, relatively well-known companies, so that foreign investors are unlikely to buy secondary and small U.S. issues. The extent of foreign investors' concentration in large famous companies is not known to me, but the following story exemplifies the idea. Supposedly, an international money management organization created a brand-name mutual fund portfolio for Japan: the portfolio owned only stocks of firms whose products could be bought in retail stores—for example, it would contain Pepsi Cola, but not United Technologies.

If a group of investors with a common orientation increase their holdings in a market, their preferred sector will increase in value, and there will be a transitory boom, unless other investors sell them the stock readily.

SHORT-TERM CYCLES IN RELATIVE VALUES OF LIQUID AND ILLIQUID STOCKS

Demand for liquid stocks as a means to gain rapid exposure to the equity market has been a third element of demand for large stocks. An investor engaged in any high-turnover, dynamic strategy will trade only in liquid stocks to minimize trading costs and execution delays. Portfolio insurance is such a strategy; portfolio insurers tend to buy stocks in a market rise, and to sell them in a market fall. When portfolio insurers choose to trade in the index futures market, instead of trading stocks directly, then arbitrageurs will do the buying and selling of the actual stocks. In this case, because the arbitrage is between an index of liquid stocks and the stocks themselves, the arbitrageur will have double reason to concentrate trades among the liquid stocks: first, because trading costs are the lowest, and second because those are the stocks in the index and so provide the closest tracking to the index. Therefore, when the market rises, portfolio insurance soon creates preferential demand for liquid stocks, and when the market falls, the same forces release a preferential supply of these stocks.

When there is net demand for liquid stocks by participants in dynamic strategies, that net demand moves the liquid part of the market above the rest of the market, until other owners of those liquid stocks are ready to sell in accommodation. Because trading costs money, prices must rise at least far enough to offset the accommodator's trading costs. Hence, there will be an increase in the relative price of these liquid stocks, relative to the prices of other stocks into which the accommodators shift when they sell the liquid names. As the net demand eases, the prices will fall back into line. If the market later falls, the net supply of liquid stocks will drive the prices of the liquid stocks down ahead of the market; hence the value of liquid stocks relative to illiquid stocks cycles on a short-term basis.

The liquid stock cycle has been clearly observable over the past year. Because of its short duration, it is an easy cycle to demonstrate. A sophisticated analysis would require a study of actual trade prices at the time of trade, but a rough indication of the effect can be obtained by comparing a small-stock oriented index like the Valueline, or a less liquid index of NASDAQ stocks, against an index of liquid, large stocks like the DJIA. (This rough study is not conclusive as regards market efficiency, because the cycle sometimes evolves over a matter of hours, and the Valueline index—which includes many stocks which have not recently traded and so exhibit lagged prices—is not a true indication of current trade prices.) When carefully observed over hourly intervals, the cycle is statistically significant. Therefore, in this one special case, at least, we may agree on the existence of a cycle in the relative valuation of market sectors.

Investor Psychology and Market Inefficiencies

Meir Statman

The typical turnover ratio for mutual funds and other managed funds exceeds 60 percent. Why do people trade so much? Perhaps they have inside information. People with inside information make money by trading with those who have only public information. But, if that is true, why don't people without inside information stop trading? The evidence on market efficiency provides a similar problem. The evidence on return anomalies suggests that there are ways to beat the market. The real puzzle is that money managers are unable to do so. I will discuss the reasons people trade without inside information and the implications for money management and market efficiency.

If money managers cannot beat the market, why do they continue trading? Moreover, why do the clients of money managers continue to employ them? Let me suggest two related answers. The first is cognitive: People mistake noise for information, and trade on noise as if it were information. The second is emotional: People like to trade because trading brings them the joy of pride.

I will begin with the cognitive area. In a classic head and shoulders pattern, technical analysts wait for the left shoulder to form, then the head, and then the right shoulder. When the right shoulder touches the neckline, they sell and make a bundle. Harry Roberts (1959) showed that the same kind of a pattern could be generated by a simulation with random numbers (see Figures 1a and 1b; the randomness is evident in Figure 1b). Roberts showed that people are subject to cognitive errors; they see patterns where randomness exists. Roberts also showed how statistical techniques may be used to distinguish patterns from randomness.

The confusion of randomness for patterns is an example of an optical illusion. Figure 2 presents a familiar optical illusion. The top line in Figure 2a seems longer than the bottom line. In fact, as shown in Figure 2b, the opposite is true. Optical illusions are special, because they do not

FIGURE 1. Simulated Market Patterns

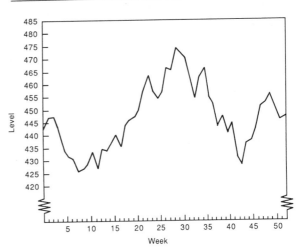

a. Simulated market levels for 52 weeks

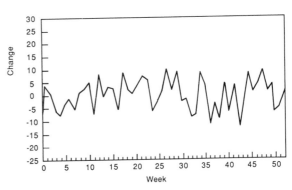

b. Simulated market changes for 52 weeks

Source: Roberts, "Stock Market Patterns and Financial Analysis: Methodological Suggestions," *Journal of Finance* (March 1959).

disappear even after you realize that they are illusions. They represent a failure of learning, blind spots in the processing of information by the brain.

Cognitive errors are not confined to optical illusions. Many people believe that there is a "hot hand" in basketball—a basketball player is more likely to score a hit after a series of hits.

FIGURE 2. Optical Illusions

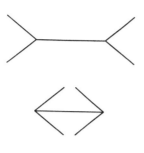

a. The Muller-Lyer Illusion

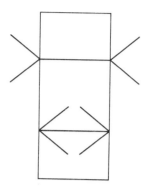

b. A transparent version of the Muller-Lyer Illusion

Source: Tversky and Kahneman, "Rational Choice and the Framing of Decisions," *Journal of Business* (59), 1986.

Players, coaches, and fans are convinced that a "hot hand" phenomenon exists, but it does not. Gilovich, Vallone, and Tversky (1985) examined the probability of scoring a hit in the second of two free throws. They found that Larry Bird of the Boston Celtics scored a hit following a miss 91 percent of the times. He scored a hit following a hit 88 percent of the time. The two figures are not statistically different (see Table 1). This and similar evidence show that the "hot hand" is an illusion. Yet players, coaches, and fans continue to believe that it is real.

Cognitive errors appear in financial contexts as well. The Sentiment Index provides an example. Investors Intelligence classifies advisers into bulls or bears, and publishes the percentage of advisers who are bearish. Figure 3 presents both the Bearish Sentiment Index and the Dow Jones Index. The two seem to move together.

Investors Intelligence and others claim that the Index serves as a contrary indicator—investors should buy when advisers are bearish and sell when they are bullish. Michael Solt and I decided to test this claim (Solt and Statman, 1987). The results of our analysis showed two things. First, the Sentiment Index follows the market: advisers become bullish after the market has gone up, and they become bearish after the market has gone down. Second, there is no systematic relationship between advisers sentiment—bullish or bearish—and the movement of the market in the subsequent period. In short, the relationship between the Sentiment Index and the market is a relationship where the market leads the Index.

The confusion between the variable that leads and the variable that follows is a form of optical illusion. As noted by Sharpe (1985):

"Occasionally the proponent of a system will produce a graph that plots both the levels of an indicator intended to predict future market moves and the levels of the market itself. Visual comparison of the two curves may suggest that the indicator has indeed predicted changes in the market. However, the eye cannot easily differentiate between a situation in which changes in a market "predictor" follow the market and one in which the changes precede the market. But the distinction is crucial, for only a

TABLE 1. Probability of making a second free throw conditioned on the outcome of the first free throw for nine members of the Boston Celtics during the 1980-1981 and 1981-1982 seasons.

Player	$P(H^2/M^1)$	$P(H^2/H^1)$	Serial Correlation r
Larry Bird	.91 (53)	.88 (285)	−.032
Cedric Maxwell	.76 (128)	.81 (302)	.061
Robert Parish	.72 (105)	.77 (213)	.056
Nate Archibald	.82 (76)	.83 (245)	.014
Chris Ford	.77 (22)	.71 (51)	−.069
Keven McHale	.59 (49)	.73 (128)	.130
M.L. Carr	.81 (26)	.68 (57)	−.128
Rick Robey	.61 (80)	.59 (91)	−.019
Gerald Henderson	.78 (37)	.76 (101)	−.022

Note: The number of shots upon which each probability is based is given in parentheses.
Source: Gilovich, Vallone, and Tversky, "The hot hand in basketball: On the misperception of random sequences," *Cognitive Psychology* (17), 1985.

situation of the latter type can bring superior investment performance (p. 608)."

Standard statistical techniques can be used to distinguish the follower from the leader, but they are not always used. People generally substitute intuitive judgment for statistical analysis, but intuitive judgment is not always good. Yet people are highly confident in their intuitive judgment. Kahneman and Tversky (1973) wrote:

"[P]eople are prone to experience much confidence in highly fallible judgment, a phenomenon that may be termed the *illusion of validity*. Like other perceptual and judgmental errors, the illusion of validity persists even when its illusory character is recognized (p. 249)."

Einhorn and Hogarth (1978) suggested that the illusion of validity persists because people focus on information that confirms their hypotheses and neglect disconfirming information. The focus on confirming evidence is illus-

trated in statements such as that by Boland (1980):

"The October Massacres of 1978 and 1979 were heralded by peaks in adviser optimism. And the November lows of both years found the tip sheets looking for lower lows (p. 11)."

Similarly, Dreman (1982) wrote:

"[A]t the market high in late 1972, 75% of advisers predicted that stocks were heading skyward. Then at the bottom of the 1974 market—the worst break in the postwar period—two-thirds suspected stocks would continue to free-fall; not long thereafter we had the beginning of a major bull market (p. 298)."

The cases presented by Boland and Dreman are hits, observations consistent with the hypothesis that the Sentiment Index is useful as a forecaster of changes in the market. But what about false positives and negatives? How fre-

FIGURE 3. The Bearish Sentiment Index and the Dow Jones Industrial Average, 1963–1985

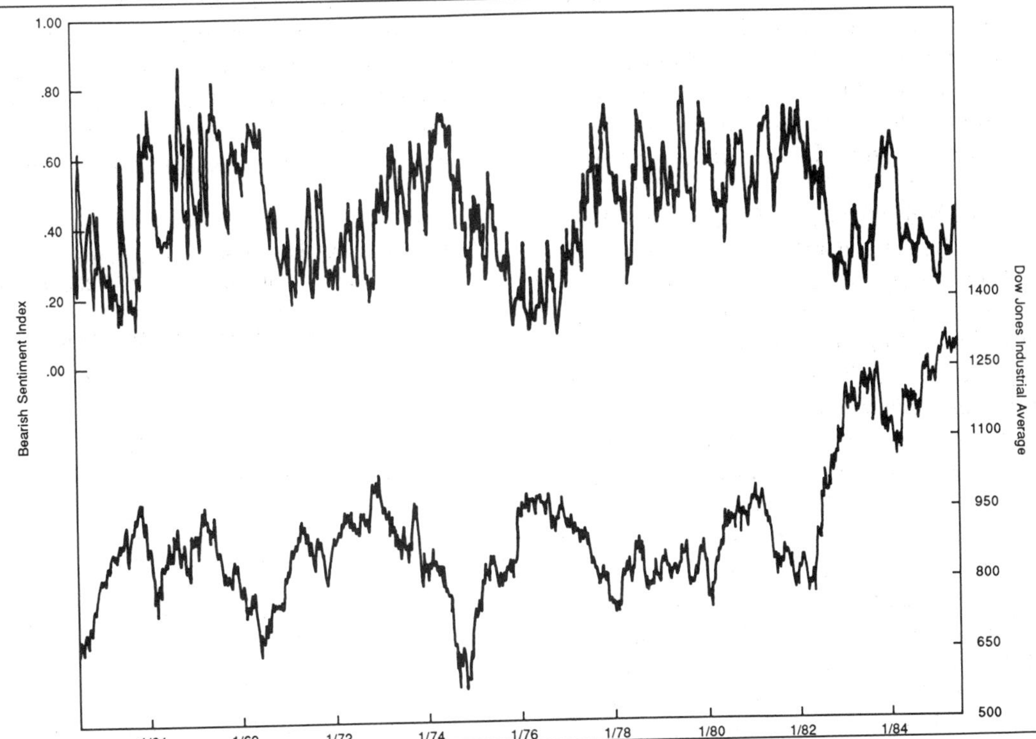

Source: Solt and Statman, "How useful is the Sentiment Index?" (Santa Clara University Working Paper, 1987).

quently did the Sentiment Index forecast an increase in the market when, in fact, a decrease followed? And how often did it forecast a decrease when, in fact, an increase followed? We found that the frequency of false positives and negatives is high. Indeed, the Index is useless, not because it does not provide some good forecasts, but because it provides so many bad forecasts.

Why do people trade? In part, people trade because they think that they have either superior information or superior information processing methods. Much of what they see as information is nothing but noise or randomness, however. Traders see patterns in stock prices that are random, and they rely on intuitive judgment even when systematic analysis would have demonstrated that their judgment is incorrect.

Cognitive errors induce people to trade, but they are not the only motivation for trades. The second motivation is emotional. Specifically, people trade because trading brings with it the joy of pride. When someone decides to buy a stock he assumes responsibility for the decision. A stock that goes up brings not only profits, but also pride. The responsibility that brings profits and the joy of pride when a decision turns out to be right, however, also brings losses and the pain of regret when it turns out to be wrong. Investors trade because they want to experience the joy of pride that accompanies a gain.

The problem with trading is that decisions might turn out to be wrong and inflict the pain of regret. Investors try to increase the amount of pride and reduce the amount of regret through several devices. One device is postponement of the realization of losses. Postponement is effective because the pain of regret is felt when a loss is realized. As Gross (1982) noted in his manual for stockbrokers:

"Many clients, however, will not sell anything at a loss. They don't want to give up the hope of making money on a particular investment, or perhaps they want to get even before they get out. The "getevenitis" disease has probably wrought more destruction on investment portfolios than anything else. Rather than recovering to an original entry price, many investments plunge sickeningly. Investors are also reluctant to accept and realize losses because the very act of doing so proves that their first judgment was wrong . . . Investors who accept losses can no longer prattle to their loved ones, "Honey, it's only a paper loss. Just wait. It will come back." Investors who realize losses must admit their folly to the IRS, when they file that itemized tax return. For all those reasons and more, investors as a whole are reluctant to take losses, even when they feel that to do so is the right course of action (p. 150)."

Another device for the reduction of regret is its transfer to full-fee stockbrokers and other investment advisers. We know that full-fee brokers and investment advisers are unable to beat the market. So why do they persist? I think they persist because they play the role of the scapegoat. Full-fee brokers sometimes complain that clients are unfair. When a stock goes up, the client says, "I bought the stock." But when a stock goes down, the client says, "My broker sold me the stock." What full-fee brokers seem to neglect is that they provide no service other than those of a scapegoat. They get paid so that their clients will be able to claim most of the pride that comes with decisions that turn out well and shift to the broker the regret that comes with decisions that did not turn out well.

Brokers are not always ignorant of the blame-shifting technique. They use it themselves. The following paragraph from Gross's manual for stockbrokers is an illustration.

"When you choose a stock for mass merchandising and big position building, restrict your choice solely to issues positively recommended as current buys on a fundamental basis by your firm. Should the stock perform badly after purchase, it's the firm's fault! It is the research department's error. It was the analyst who judged incorrectly! You can legitimately direct the customer's ire away from you toward several other sources. You and the client can jointly deplore the bad outcome and still retain a decent relationship, and perhaps the hope of recovery by means of a different analyst's suggestion (p. 180)."

The emotional reason for trading is linked with the cognitive reason. First, investors must believe that they have a way to beat the market.

Otherwise, they ascribe both gains and losses to luck and do not take responsibility for their choices. Without responsibility there is not pain of regret, but neither is there the joy of pride. Investors who believe that markets are efficient buy and hold, and their investment life is emotionally boring. Those who believe that they can beat the market using public information, and those who hire investment advisers to help them beat the market, must deceive themselves into believing that the advisers are experts, not scapegoats. Self-deception is rather common and not unique to the investment arena. For example, Rolls Royce owners probably believe that they bought their cars because of the high quality. Others suspect that the main reason for the purchase is a display of wealth.

The desire to transfer blame leads investors to regard their advisers as experts and obscures the perception of their role as scapegoats. Now imagine that I offered you a deal: "Pay me $10 and I will shoulder all responsibility for your decisions that go wrong." That would be silly. You cannot transfer blame to a scapegoat when you recognize him as a scapegoat. You can transfer responsibility and blame only when you believe that an investment adviser qualifies as an expert.

Shifting responsibility and blame to an adviser is a good defense against regret, but now the adviser must bear the blame and suffer the pain of regret. Bearing the pain of regret may be the relative advantage of investment advisers, but no one likes the pain of regret. Choosing "quality" stocks is an effective way to reduce regret. It is described well in the following paragraph from the manual for stockbrokers by Gross:

"You will be able to sleep better at night as a merchandiser of quality stock shares. Your own self-respect is a fragile but necessary ingredient that can best be preserved through knowing you are a purveyor of quality. When clients lose money, you will suffer along with them, but your distress will be less if you have full knowledge that a profit was sought with a prudent eye toward quality. When high quality investments lose value, their holders are less likely to litigate, by the way, than they would be with similar losses in low-rated issues. Investors who lose money on high quality issues frequently direct their anger more toward the market than toward the broker who recommended the stock. Investors who lose on low quality issues tend to direct their anger toward the broker, and they may seek redress through court action (p. 176)."

Some choices involve less responsibility than others. For example, a failure with a stock such as IBM is an "act of God" and no one could be held responsible for it; but a failure with the stock of a company of low reputation involves much responsibility and high potential for regret. If so, we should find that stocks of companies with high reputations provide lower expected returns than stocks of companies with low reputations. The higher returns on stocks of companies with low reputations are compensation for regret, analogous to compensation for risk. *Fortune* magazine publishes surveys of companies by reputation, and preliminary analysis indicates that the hypothesis holds. Moreover, it is possible that well-known anomalies such as those associated with price/earnings, book/price, and neglect are merely manifestations of compensation for bearing regret.

In summary, people trade for both cognitive and emotional reasons. They trade because they think that they have information when they have nothing but noise, and they trade because trading can bring the joy of pride. Trading brings pride when decisions turn out well, but it brings regret when decisions do not turn out well. Investors try to avoid the pain of regret by avoiding the realization of losses, employing investment advisers as scapegoats, and avoiding stocks of companies with low reputations.

Question and Answer Session

QUESTION: Is the small firm effect cyclical?

ROSENBERG: The theme of this presentation is that to justify naming periods "cycles," it is not enough that the prices go up and down; they must go up and down for a reason that is not explained by the intrinsic value of the companies in the two sectors. Thus, the answer to this question depends on a comparison of sector values to sector prices. I would be very interested to see the results.

QUESTION: Do you find any evidence of market cycles in stocks versus bonds?

ROSENBERG: That is a very difficult question to analyze conclusively: so many factors can legitimately influence bond and stock values—especially long-term prospects for interest rates and for economic activity—that it is difficult to find a reliable indication of underlying value. Recently, bonds have severely underperformed stocks, and it is interesting to ask if they will soon reverse.[1] I can only point out that the high correlation between the bond and stock markets for the 1980s through 1986 is not necessarily a permanent phenomenon. For the United States, across the five decades through 1978, the correlation between long-term government bond returns and stock returns was small and almost insignificant. The correlation rose in the 1980s, as we moved into a monetarist period and interest rates became more volatile. Someone who grew up when I did would not be surprised to see the bond market and the stock market diverge sharply. But because of the short-term correlation that has characterized the two markets recently, which has been very strong and highly consistent, people have come to expect that the correlation will continue.

QUESTION: With the increased interest in quantitative analysis, how do you explain the poor performance this year by "quant" stocks, as pointed out recently by the *Wall Street Journal*?

[1] Editorial Note: They did reverse in the very next month, October 1987.

ROSENBERG: I do not think that the *Wall Street Journal* necessarily knows what a "quantitative stock" is—I certainly do not. People who use quantitative methods should come up with different conclusions as to which stocks to buy, just as traditional investors differ in their conclusions. It is better to speak of "quantitative managers" than of "quantitative stocks." At my firm, our portfolios are ahead of their bogies by 50 basis points so far this year, which seems to contradict the article you cite. To be more responsive to your question, high-yield stocks did very badly so far this year in comparison to other stocks. This is to be expected when the bond market underperforms the stock market, because utilities and financial stocks have bond-like characteristics, and high-yield stocks in general have a high residual correlation with the bond market. Net of the bond market impact, those high-yield stocks probably just about matched the stock market. A fairly high proportion of quantitative managers have a strong yield tilt in their equity portfolios, and can be expected to perform badly when the bond market does badly. This does not necessarily have anything to do with quantitative management per se.

QUESTION: What are the implications of risk and reward preferences for gambling on investment behavior?

STATMAN: There is evidence that people tend to prefer bets on the long shots and that these are the worst bets. This preference is most pronounced at the end of the day. People take risky bets in an attempt to "break even" and avoid the regret that comes when losses are realized.

QUESTION: Does your work depend on investor focus on individual stocks rather than on portfolio risk?

STATMAN: The fact is, people do focus on individual stocks rather than on the portfolio as a whole. People are not as diversified as they should be. Look at window-dressing. If people focus on portfoliios, why would they care about the individual stocks that make up the portfolio?

QUESTION: Is "disgustingness" a market sector? What duration of returns to the "yuck" factor should we expect? And is "yuck" a legitimate risk measure?

ROSENBERG: In a society like ours, where you can make something of anything, it is hard to think that "yuck" would be a permanent factor of return, because people would be very proud then of being yuckers. In fact, they would wear T-shirts that said, "Buy yuck and win." In a culture which assumes that excellence will be rewarded, however, it might be very different. I also think that neglect is different from yuck.

Neglect is simply a lack of perception. There have been a lot of studies about this, however they are not conclusive, because neglected companies seem also to be small companies—almost a perfect correlation—or privately-held companies, or companies that fell out of the database. But the general idea that a neglected company could be rewarded simply because it is neglected makes sense. In other words, the easiest error to make is an error of omission by money managers. But the statistical evidence is not very strong. In fact, to the extent that there have been studies of neglect as distinct from other factors those studies have not shown any reward for neglect. As distinct from being small, neglected stocks have not done any better than other small stocks.

Disentangling Equity Return Regularities

Bruce I. Jacobs and Kenneth N. Levy, CFA

For decades, the efficient market hypothesis was a central paradigm in finance. In recent years, however, there has been a proliferation of empirical results uncovering anomalous security pricing behavior. Departures from conventional theory are generally referred to as anomalies, or in the case of stock market anomalies, as return regularities. This session will review the anomaly literature, present some of the research done at Jacobs Levy Equity Management, and explore some investment strategies consistent with our findings. As indicated by the title of this presentation, the "disentangling" or "purifying" of equity return regularities will be a predominant theme.

First, let us examine the evolution of common stock strategies, with particular attention to the influence of academic thought. Prior to 1970, the investment norm was traditional security analysis and stock picking. But by 1970, the notion of the random walk and the efficient market hypothesis (EMH) was being disseminated; by 1977, the EMH had substantial empirical support. At that time, indexed funds were a revolutionary product and a natural outgrowth of the efficient market hypothesis.

By 1978, however, there was growing empirical evidence of contradictions to the efficient market hypothesis. Some of these return effects had long been part of market folklore. Regularities were identified, some of which were cross-sectional and others of which were time-dependent in nature. For instance, the price/earnings (P/E) effect was documented by Basu (1979), and the size effect by Banz (1981). Time-dependent regularities included the day-of-the-week and January effects.

A number of academic researchers attempted to explain away the return regularities with critiques of methodology. Deficiencies in risk measurement were often cited. For instance, it was hypothesized that infrequent trading caused underestimation of risk as measured by beta. Although adjustments were made for this bias, it failed to explain anomalous returns. Despite close scrutiny, anomalies persisted, and the efficient market hypothesis began to crumble.

In recent years, a pervasive web of interrelated anomalies has been revealed. Most recent research, however, focuses simultaneously on at most two or three anomalies—such as the size, P/E, and neglect effects. Such an approach is insufficient for fully disentangling, or purifying, the effects. In the process of disentangling we find substantial evidence contravening market efficiency. The weight of recent empirical evidence has buried the EMH.

Anomalies are also robust to current theoretical asset pricing models. Neither the capital asset pricing model (CAPM) nor the arbitrage pricing theory (APT) can account for many of the observed return regularities. Nevertheless, new theories are beginning to emerge which offer some clues as to why anomalies exist. Today, in the absence of adequate descriptive theory, empiricism reigns supreme; and some new investment approaches are beginning to evolve. We are going to review some of these anomalies.

VALUE-BASED REGULARITIES

The value-based anomalies include returns associated with low price/book ratios, low price/sales, low price/cashflow, low P/E, and dividend yield. These regularities are, of course, related. For instance, stocks with low price/book ratios are also likely to have low price/sales ratios. In fact, the correlation between these two ratios across stocks is 0.45. The degree of relatedness is referred to as collinearity, or multicollinearity for several variables.

The low P/E effect refers to the empirical regularity that low P/E stocks tend to outperform the average. These stocks are often perceived as risky because the companies are not highly regarded. Another regularity is the dividend yield effect which is associated with tax laws. Capital gains may be deferred, and until recently were taxed at lower rates than dividends. Thus, taxable investors demand a higher pretax return on high-yield stocks to compensate for the increased tax liability. The actual payoff is U-shaped, with both high-yielding and zero-yielding stocks having the largest returns.

EARNINGS EXPECTATIONS-BASED REGULARITIES

The most familiar earnings expectations-based regularity is the neglected-firm effect. Firm neglect may be measured by institutional ownership or by the number of security analysts following a stock.

The trends-in-analysts'-estimates effect refers to the observation that stocks whose earnings have been recently upgraded tend to outperform the averages. This phenomenon was initially attributed to inefficient information propagation, but then it was noticed that these trends seem to persist over time. Alternatively, this finding may be caused by the herd instinct of Wall Street analysts—that is, when one analyst revises, the others tend to follow suit. Or it may be caused by the preference of analysts for small revisions, as they are often averse to reversing forecasts.

The earnings-surprise effect refers to the tendency for stocks to outperform following a positive earnings surprise. Earnings surprise is defined as reported earnings exceeding consensus expectations. The dispersion of analysts' estimates is a measure of uncertainty for which investors may demand compensation.

The earnings-torpedo effect has been popularized by Bob Hagin.[1] It represents the bias of analysts to be overly optimistic for successful companies and overly pessimistic for unsuccessful ones. Earnings surprises in high-expectation stocks tend to be negative surprises, hence the term "torpedoes." On the other hand, low-expectation stocks often report pleasant surprises.

Late earnings reporters are often companies deferring the release of bad news. A strategy of preemptively selling such issues may avoid negative hits.

[1] See Dr. Hagin's presentation, pp. 16—20.

PRICE-BASED REGULARITIES

Another set of regularities are price-based. These are often considered to be technical measures or potential violators of weak form efficiency. The simplest of these regularities is the price-per-share effect: Low-price stocks tend to outperform high-price stocks. In fact, some have found that this holds true even after accounting for bid-asked spreads.

Market capitalization is another price-based regularity. Everyone knows that small cap stocks have had historically strong performance. These stocks tend to be relatively illiquid and underresearched stocks; they also tend to be lower in price.

Some price-based regularities are associated with risk. We consider three measures of risk: beta, sigma, and co-skewness. The capital asset pricing model (CAPM) suggests that beta, or systematic risk, is compensated with higher return. Residual risk, or sigma, is not compensated in the CAPM framework. It may be, however, that sigma should earn additional return, possibly because investors are not well diversified; hence, they are averse to residual risk. Co-skewness is related to the degree of asymmetry in a return distribution. Investors may prefer stocks having positive co-skewness with market returns.

There is also evidence of return regularities to various measures of price momentum. The residual reversal effect—the tendency for recent performance to reverse over the short run—appears to be a strong pocket of inefficiency. For instance, if General Motors and Chrysler were up 10 percent last week while Ford was up only 2 percent, portfolio managers might tend to buy the latter name. Hence, Ford might catch up.

In the intermediate run, relative strength works in a positive fashion, as practitioners have long maintained. But recent research indicates that stock prices tend to reverse over long cycles: The biggest losers over the past three to five years tend to be the biggest gainers over the next three to five years (DeBondt and Thaler, 1985, and Fama and French, 1987).

Finally, the interaction between tax effects and past prices must be considered. For instance, stocks that are depressed near year-end are more likely to be sold for tax-loss recognition in that year and tend to bounce back early in the new year. On the other hand, stocks that have run-up in price are often not sold until the new year to defer gain recognition, and consequently are under selling pressure in the new year.

CALENDAR-BASED REGULARITIES

The next set of regularities are calendar-based.[2] Yale Hirsh's *Stock Trader's Almanac* is a treasure trove of such effects. At the short end of the time spectrum, there is the time-of-day effect. With the advent of real-time, computer-readable data, it has been documented that returns do not simply follow a clock-time or a trading-time pattern; rather, there exist both return and volatility regularities. The day-of-the-week effect, also known as the Blue Monday effect or the weekend effect, refers to the tendency of prices to close the week strong and to open the week soft. This may be related to the tendency of companies to announce bad news after the close, especially over weekends. Even the SEC has recently contributed to this anomaly. Witness the recent string of insider trading indictments. The SEC held off announcing these indictments until after the close on Fridays.

There is also a week-of-the-month effect. The first two weeks of a month tend to experience positive market returns, while the last two weeks are on average flat. This may relate to the tendency to release good news early and the proclivity to delay announcing bad news. Earnings announcements during the first two weeks of each month have been found to be generally positive and, during the last two weeks, less so. Finally, there is a month-of-the-year effect, also known as the January effect. January is a good performance month, perhaps for tax-related reasons, as was documented as early as 1942. The January effect is multifaceted: many anomalies, such as the size and yield effects, appear to have January seasonals.

ANOMALY INTERRELATIONSHIPS

The anomalies identified above are not necessarily independent effects. Figure 1 illustrates some previously documented anomaly interrelationships. Displayed is a web of relationships between some calendar-based, some price-based, and some value-based anomalies.

Price and value-based anomalies, shown in the lower part of the diagram all have price in their definition. Hence, they would be expected

to have somewhat correlated payoffs. For instance, studies have shown that the rates of return that accrue to lower-priced stocks are about the same in magnitude as those that accrue to smaller-sized firms; but the real question is: Do these effects exist independently?

The size and P/E interrelationship has been researched substantially, with conflicting results as to which anomaly really matters. Investors, who consider themselves to be low P/E investors, may be benefiting from the high book/price effect. The unusual return to zero-yielding stocks has been shown to be independent of their lower price or smaller size.

There are also relationships between calendar-based regularities and price and value-based regularities. For instance, let us examine the January effect. Researchers have found that much of the size effect takes place in the last calendar day in December, plus the first few days in January. It has also been found that the U-shaped payoff to yield, which is the payoff to both zero- and high-yielding stocks, tends to occur in January: Returns to the yield attribute are completely flat during the rest of the year. Keim (1987) finds evidence that two-thirds of the size effect occurs on Friday. Also, the time-of-the-day effect depends upon the day-of-the-week, and the day-of-the-week effect may be different in January.

Most previous research is limited to sorting out two or at most three anomalies jointly. This is not sufficient. Let me illustrate with an example from the medical profession. What variables should one use to study the determinants of a person's blood pressure? Should the explanatory variables arbitrarily be limited to just two? Perhaps just marital status and years of education? Other factors—such as exercise, diet, and income—are clearly important. A study draw-

[2] For an elaboration of these effects see B. Jacobs and K. Levy (1988).

FIGURE 1. Some Anomaly Interrelationships

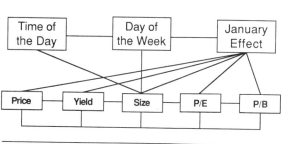

Source: Jacobs Levy Equity Management

ing conclusions based on only two explanatory variables could yield highly misleading results.

The same is true for stock market anomalies. There have been several studies that conclusively proved that size subsumes P/E; that is, after controlling for size, there is no remaining P/E effect. There are as many studies that prove just the opposite. Others believe that size and P/E do not matter at all; instead, neglect matters. Another alternative is that all three effects exist independently.

It is fair to say that some of these conflicting findings may be caused by different methodological techniques, different time periods, or different data samples. Nevertheless, if one wants to understand the marketplace fully, these effects must be fully disentangled and purified. In our research, we disentangle 25 anomaly measures simultaneously, which facilitates a much clearer view of the marketplace.

FIGURE 2. P/E vs. Size: Monthly Returns (%)

Small Size				Large Size
1.55	1.45	1.20	1.07	0.89
1.56	1.12	1.12	0.98	0.59
1.19	1.08	0.85	0.71	0.46
1.37	0.83	0.61	0.62	0.52
1.23	1.05	0.68	0.76	0.48

(Rows labeled Low P/E at top, High P/E at bottom)

Source: S. Basu, *Journal of Financial Economics*, 1983.

There are several methods for disentangling anomalies. Figure 2 illustrates a two-way classification scheme. This method is taken from a study by Basu (1983). Basu formed 25 portfolios by dividing the sample into quintiles on the basis of size, and then on the basis of P/E ratios. The figure seems to reveal independent effects. For instance, looking across the rows, there seems to be a size effect; down the columns, there seems to be a low P/E effect. Although initially it appeared that both effects existed, Basu went on to randomize the experimental design and to control for risk; and in so doing, he concluded that P/E subsumes size.

FIGURE 3. P/E vs. Size vs. Neglect: Three-Way Classification

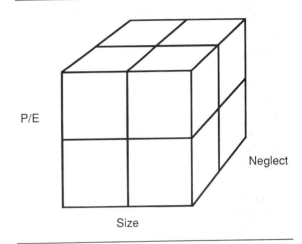

Source: Jacobs Levy Equity Management

The classification scheme may be generalized for additional anomalies. For instance, Figure 3 illustrates a three-way classification ranked high or low on the P/E, size, and neglect measures, which results in eight portfolios. As more anomalies are added, however, this approach becomes somewhat unmanageable—that is, there would not be enough observations per cell for meaningful samples, and there would be far too many cells for interpretation. For instance, if we quintile on each of 25 anomaly measures, we would produce a 25-dimensional Rubik's cube with 3×10^{17} cells. Using a procedure for analyzing monthly returns on 1,500 stocks, it would take 17 trillion years to accumulate just one observation per cell.

There is another approach, however, which is similar in spirit to the multifactor risk approach pioneered by *BARRA*. A simple univariate regression of stock excess return on one anomaly at a time can be run. The method is shown in Table 1 for the size effect. The slope coefficient 'C' represents the payoff to the size anomaly. This payoff will be biased by omitted

TABLE 1. Anomaly Regression Models

Univariate Model (Naive):

$$R_i - R_f = A + (C * SIZE_i) + E_i$$

Multivariate model (Pure):

$$R_i - R_f = A + SUM_j [C_j * ANOMALY_j] + SUM_k [D_k * OTHER\ ATTRIBUTES_{ik}] + E_i$$

Source: Jacobs Levy Equity Management

attributes correlated with size, such as P/E and industry affiliation. Hence, we refer to it as a naive payoff, since it naively assumes that size is unrelated to other effects.

Alternatively, multivariate regression may be used to estimate all return effects simultaneously. The right-hand side of the equation controls for other anomalies and other attributes, such as industry affiliation. This regression results in a set of payoff coefficients, c_j, which represents the incremental return contribution of each anomaly. We refer to these as pure payoffs, because each payoff is purified of other effects. For example, the payoff for size is purified of returns associated with other attributes, such as the tendency for larger companies to have higher yields or to be more oil-related than smaller companies.

RESEARCH RESULTS

Jacobs Levy Equity Management recently completed a major research project on anomalies. The study examined a total of 25 anomaly measures and 38 industries simultaneously, using monthly multivariate regressions on the 1,500 largest companies for the 108-month period from January 1978 to December 1986. In so doing, we were able to fully disentangle and measure the various cross-currents in the equity market during this period.

Table 2 shows the average monthly returns to selected anomalies. The numbers represent returns to a one cross-sectional standard deviation of exposure to each attribute. This is roughly equivalent to a 16th percentile ranking, so these returns represent a payoff to a very substantial attribute exposure, which we will refer to as one unit of exposure. The first column shows the average of monthly naive payoffs to each measure. The second column shows the average of monthly pure payoffs to each measure.

The results indicate that the three anomalies discussed earlier—low P/E, small size, and neglect—do all exist in their naive form. The payoff to low P/E is 59 basis points on average per month, to small size 15 basis points, and to neglect 14 basis points. But do these anomalies merely proxy one for the other? The pure results show that all three effects exist independently. Moreover, because these are pure effects, they are fully additive. Furthermore, the pure payoffs, although slightly smaller than the naive

TABLE 2. Average Monthly Returns To Selected Anomalies (in percent)

Anomaly	Naive	Pure
Low Price/Earnings	.59**	.46**
Small Size	.15*	.12**
Neglect	.14*	.10*
Residual Reversal	−.54**	−1.08a
Cash Flow/Price	.36**	.04

*10% confidence
**1% confidence
a) T-Statistic = −17.8
Source: Jacobs Levy Equity Management

payoffs, tend to be more statistically significant. This occurs because a slight reduction in strength of the purified returns is more than compensated for by an increase in their consistency of payoff over time.

We also find that the residual reversal effect is quite strong, as shown in Table 2. This coefficient is negative, which indicates that stocks which perform well in one month tend to underperform in the next. In this case, the pure returns are twice as strong as the naive returns; the t-statistic is also quite high. It seems that this outcome could not be due to chance. One reason that the pure returns are much stronger than the naive returns is that we have disentangled for related measures such as earnings surprise. For example, if a stock outperforms one month, it is likely to underperform the next. But if last month's pop is due to a positive earnings surprise or a positive earnings estimate revision, then it is more likely that the performance will persist and not reverse.

The fifth anomaly presented in Table 2 is cashflow/price. This particular anomaly may be illusory. It provides 36 basis points of average monthly return in naive form, but it is almost completely dissipated in pure form. Cashflow/price is highly correlated with other attributes such as P/E and book/price ratios. When these attributes are included in the multivariate regression, the cashflow/price effect vanishes.

It is insufficient to look only at average monthly returns; the month-by-month variation must also be examined. Figure 4 illustrates the cumulative pure returns to low P/E. An average can indeed mask a multitude of sins. Low P/E investing has not been particularly desirable in recent months. On the other hand, if one had maintained a one unit exposure to low P/E over the entire period, with neutral or zero exposure to all of the other measures, one would have

FIGURE 4. Cumulative Return to Low P/E

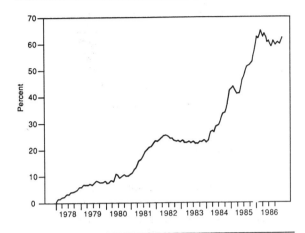

Source: Jacobs Levy Equity Management

outperformed the market by 60 percent, before transactions costs. Cumulative pure returns to the small size attribute are illustrated in Figure 5. Again, small size has not performed particularly well since 1984. On the other hand, over the entire period, there was approximately a 14 percent advantage.

Figures 4 and 5 show that the returns to anomalies are not constant over time. They may be nonstationary, which means that their trends and variabilities may change over time.

Figure 6 illustrates cumulative returns following revisions in consensus earnings estimates. There are three separate measures—one-month ago, two-months ago, and three-months ago—but obviously they are highly correlated.

FIGURE 5. Cumulative Return to Small Size

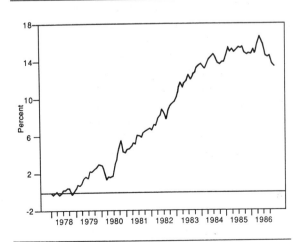

Source: Jacobs Levy Equity Management

FIGURE 6. Cumulative Return to Trends in Earnings Estimates

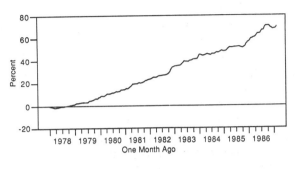

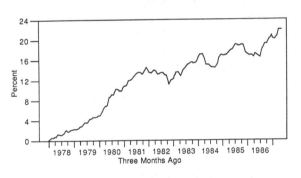

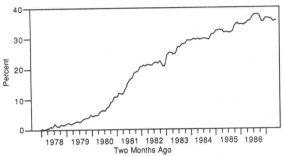

Source: Jacobs Levy Equity Management

The figure shows that the return is substantial for each of these three measures, but weakens over time. The outperformance would have been 70 percent over this period for lag-one revisions, 35 percent for lag-two revisions, and 20 percent for lag-three revisions. Since these effects are purified, they are independent; hence they are fully additive. If, over this period, a portfolio had simultaneously maintained one unit of exposure to each of these measures, total outperformance, gross of transaction costs, would have been 125 percent.

Cumulative returns to residual reversal are shown in Figure 7. Because this is a very short-lived measure, such a strategy requires substantial portfolio rebalancing to capture the excess

FIGURE 7. Cumulative Return to Residual Reversal

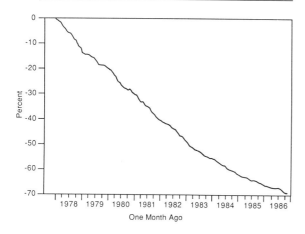

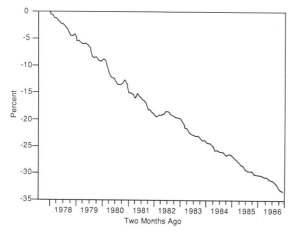

Source: Jacobs Levy Equity Management

FIGURE 8. Cumulative Return to Beta

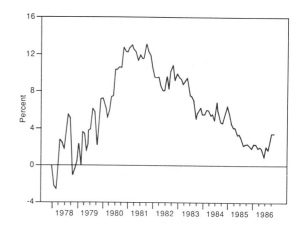

Source: Jacobs Levy Equity Management

return. A bet each month on the previous month's winners would have underperformed by 70 percent, cumulatively. On the other hand, last month's laggards would have outperformed by the same amount. A comparison of the two charts shown in the figure reveals that the two-month ago measure is about half as strong as the one-month ago measure. We classify this effect as a true pocket of market inefficiency because it is remarkably consistent. In fact, this measure works 95 percent of the time over this period.

Figure 8 illustrates cumulative pure returns to beta. This chart is particularly interesting. Early in the period, there was positive outperformance associated with the beta attribute; but later on, the performance was negative, despite the fact that we were in a strong bull market. Of course, these results may differ from other stud-

ies, because of our control for other attributes correlated with beta. The fact that pure returns to beta do not accumulate positively during such a strong bull market casts some doubt on the CAPM.

THE JANUARY EFFECT

There is evidence of January seasonals for returns to a variety of attributes. For example, approximately half of the size effect seems to occur in the month of January, and the entire U-shaped yield effect occurs in the month of January. One plausible explanation is that these effects proxy for year-end tax-loss selling. Another possibility is "window-dressing," as portfolio managers unload their embarrassing stocks at year-end, so that they do not appear on the annual holdings report.

Academics tend to dismiss such explanations, because truly repetitive patterns could be anticipated and arbitraged away. Also, if investors are rational, tax laws should not lead to any unusual year-end market activity. Short-term losses were more valuable as tax shelters than long-term losses before the 1986 tax reform. Therefore, it should have been optimal for taxable investors to sell their losers just prior to their becoming long-term in nature, rather than waiting until year-end—an artificial calendar date—to transact. But investors do not necessarily behave as rationally as conventional theory postulates. Behavioral models, like those put forth by Meir Statman, may hold the key to

TABLE 3. January vs. Rest-of-Year Returns (in percent)

	Naive		Pure	
Anomaly	Jan	Non Jan	Jan	Non Jan
Short-Term Tax-Loss	1.06	−.19*	.38	−.08
Long-Term Tax-Loss	1.43	−.44**	.78	−.07**
Book/Price	.97	.10*	.51	.05*
Small Size	.57	.11*	.14	.12
Controversy	.89	−.44*	−.01	−.06
Yield	.25	−.03	.67	−.03**
Zero Yield	1.42	−.13	1.00	.08*

* 10% significance for Jan versus Non-Jan
** 1% significance for Jan versus Non-Jan
Source: Jacobs Levy Equity Management

understanding some of the anomalous pricing behavior we have discussed.[3]

Because of the controversy surrounding January effects, we tested for the existence of January seasonals. Table 3 shows January and non-January average returns to a variety of measures in both naive and pure form. The first two measures, short-term tax-loss and long-term tax-loss, are proprietary models of pent-up tax-loss selling pressure for each stock. The other measures listed have exhibited seasonals in previous researchers' work. The naive results confirm what others have found: There are January seasonals to these particular measures. For example, small size returns 57 basis points on average in January, versus only 11 basis points in other months. Unfortunately, when one looks at the naive results, it is very hard to understand what is happening. Consider a stock that has recently declined in price. Such a stock may have embedded tax losses for both long- and short-term shareholders. In addition, it is now higher in book/price and smaller in size than it was recently; its earnings prospects may be more controversial; it may have omitted a dividend and is now a zero-yielding stock. So in examining just one attribute at a time, it is difficult to understand what is motivating that stock's behavior.

The pure returns to these effects present a different picture. There still are substantial bounce-backs for both short- and long-term tax-losses in the month of January. The payoff to the long-term measure, however, is twice the magnitude of the short-term measure, 78 basis points versus 38 basis points, and is more sig-

[3] See Dr. Statman's presentation, pp. 29–33.

nificant. This seems to contradict the idea that short-term losses are more valuable tax-shelters than long-term losses; hence, one might expect the short-term bounce-back to be stronger than the long-term bounce-back. The results are consistent with Meir Statman's proposition that people are embarrassed by their losers and have a tendency to hold them too long (Shefrin and Statman, 1985). Aside from tax issues, there is no reason to expect January seasonals for the rest of these attributes. In fact, the January seasonal dissipates completely for the small size and controversy effects when we purify returns by controlling for other attributes. Also, the January seasonal for book/price is only about half the magnitude of what it was in the naive framework, although it is still significant. On the other hand, both high-yielding and zero-yielding stocks have more significant January seasonals once we purify. Thus, this U-shaped yield effect remains a puzzle, even in the multivariate framework.

AUTOCORRELATION OF TIME-SERIES RETURNS

In addition to studying monthly patterns, the time dimension can be explored by examining the time-series correlation, or autocorrelation, of pure returns to a variety of anomaly measures. Autocorrelations are a measure of memory in the time-series process—that is, whether past returns have predictive power for future returns. If there is no memory, the process is said to be random, and we would expect all the autocorrelations to be close to zero. The Nth order autocorrelation of a time-series—for example, returns to small size—is defined as the covariance between returns to small size in month t and month t-N, divided by the variance of returns to size. Alternatively, it can be calculated as a slope coefficient from a regression of returns in month t on returns in month t-N.

Autocorrelations may reveal patterns in the time-series of returns. Figure 9 is a correlogram showing autocorrelations of pure returns to our sigma measure for various lag lengths. Observations that fall outside of the dotted corridor, either above or below it, would be significant at the 5 percent level. In this example, most of the lags between one and twelve months are statistically significant and positive.

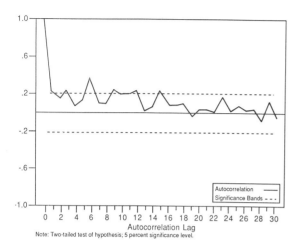

FIGURE 9. Autocorrelations of Returns to Sigma

1.0
.6
.2
-.2
-.6
-1.0
    0 2 4 6 8 10 12 14 16 18 20 22 24 26 28 30
                Autocorrelation Lag

Autocorrelation ——
Significance Bands - - -

Note: Two-tailed test of hypothesis; 5 percent significance level.

Source: Jacobs Levy Equity Management

Autocorrelations have been used to test market efficiency. As Gary Schlarbaum pointed out in his presentation, early studies of market efficiency examined the total return stock-by-stock over a period of time, looking for autocorrelation patterns; and they generally found nothing.[4] Most studies of attribute autocorrelations use naive returns to these effects. Hence, autocorrelations may be induced by omitted variable bias because the various effects are not fully disentangled. The results are different, however, for autocorrelations on components of returns, such as returns just to the size attribute.

Rosenberg and Rudd (1982) published a study which analyzed autocorrelation patterns of the total common-factor component of returns, stock by stock using a multifactor framework. They found significant first-order, common-factor correlations although no higher-order patterns. In their study, Rosenberg and Rudd aggregated all factors for each stock up to the total common factor level.

We used a different method; we tested for first, second, and higher order patterns for each anomaly individually. Our results showed many instances of first-order autocorrelations, as well as some higher-order patterns.

There are at least three possible explanations for these findings. The first explanation, changing risk premia, may be consistent with the EMH. Autocorrelations can be induced if

[4] See Dr. Schlarbaum's presentation, pp. 8–15.

risk premia and associated expected returns to attributes change over time—that is, if they are time-varying. Because risk premia generally change slowly over time, higher-order patterns would result, such as those shown in Figure 9. Most of the patterns that we have identified, however, are not higher-order. Therefore, the observed autocorrelation patterns are generally inconsistent with the EMH.

The other two explanations are also inconsistent with market efficiency. These are nonsynchronous stock response and lagged responses to macroeconomic shocks. The nonsynchronous stock explanation is illustrated with the following example. Suppose a corporate raider identifies an oil company selling at a significant discount to book value. The raider buys the company, restructures it, and sells off the pieces, reaping a windfall profit. Almost immediately, there will be speculation on other oil companies selling at book/price discounts; eventually, interest is going to spread to other natural resource companies and then perhaps to all companies selling at attractive book/price ratios. In this scenario, one might observe a period in which returns to book/price are above average. Hence, returns to book/price would not be random; rather, autocorrelations would be induced.

The third explanation is investor underestimation of the persistence of macroeconomic forces. In the last five years, trends in the U.S. dollar, oil prices, the stock market, interest rates, and inflation have all consistently overshot most expert opinion. If, for example, small companies have more ability to pass through inflation to their customers than do larger firms, and if unexpected inflation has long persistent trends, so will returns to the size effect.

MACROECONOMIC FORCES

The linkages between returns to attributes and broad macroeconomic forces can be analyzed. The earlier figures showed instability in the returns to some attributes. Perhaps this instability is due to the market climate. To investigate this possibility, we regressed both naive and pure returns to a variety of anomaly attributes on returns to the stock market.

Table 4 shows both the average return in a month when the market is flat (intercept) and the sensitivity to market returns (slope). First, consider low P/E. The naive results seem to

TABLE 4. Regression of Anomaly Returns on Market Returns

Anomaly	Naive		Pure	
	Intercept	Slope	Intercept	Slope
Low Price/Earnings	.66**	−.11**	.46**	.00
Yield	.13	−.23**	.06	−.05**
Beta	−.21	.33a	−.09	.21b
Relative Strength	.15	.17**	.28**	.09**
Residual Reversal	−.53**	−.01	−1.08c	−.01

**1% significance
a) T-Statistic = 10.7
b) T-Statistic = 9.7
c) T-Statistic = 17.5
Source: Jacobs Levy Equity Management

confirm the conventional wisdom that low P/E stocks perform relatively better in down markets than in up markets: The intercept is 66 basis points and the slope is −11 basis points, both of which are significant. For pure returns, the intercept is still significant, but the slope is not. Pure returns to low P/E are insensitive to market movements, which is consistent with Figure 4. Note that during the mid-1982 to mid-1983 bull market, low P/E strategies hurt returns, whereas during the recent mid-1983 to mid-1985 bull market, low P/E strategies paid off. This corroborates the finding that there is no clear linkage between pure returns to low P/E and returns to the overall stock market.

On the other hand, the yield measure is defensive in both naive and pure forms, as indicated by the significant negative slopes in Table 4. Thus, the observed defensive nature of low P/E in its naive form may occur because it is proxying for other measures, such as yield.

Beta is strongly procyclical; it has extremely positive and significant slopes in both naive and pure forms. The intercepts, however, are negative. This result helps to explain the lack of return accumulation to beta documented earlier in Figure 8. During this period, the negative intercept completely offsets the positive responsiveness of beta to the bull market.

Relative strength has positive intercepts and positive slopes in both naive and pure forms. This indicates that relative strength usually performs well, and it works even better in strong market environments.

Finally, the power of the residual reversal measure appears entirely in the intercept term, which roughly doubles in magnitude in pure form. The slope in both cases is trivial. This is consistent with Figure 7, which shows that residual reversal performed well over the entire period. Evidently, this is an anomaly for all seasons. Because several pure anomalies, in addition to historical beta, have significant market-related slope coefficients, a stock's future beta can be predicted better by incorporating these sensitivities. We also find that the multifactor CAPM is not a satisfactory explanation of anomalies.

The overall stock market represents only one macroeconomic "driver" that buffets returns to attributes. Other macroeconomic measures, such as interest rates and GNP, also have an impact on these returns.

CONCLUSION

Several conclusions may be drawn from this research. First, the efficient market hypothesis is challenged. The strength and consistency of our earnings surprise and trend in analysts' estimate measures seem to contravene semi-strong efficiency, because this information is in the public domain. The power of our relative strength and residual reversal measures fly in the face of weak-form efficiency, in that these measures are based solely on past prices. Some measures, such as residual reversal, seem to be true anomalous pockets of market inefficiency. Other measures, such as size and low P/E, may be anomalous or might represent "empirical return regularities" only in a broader macroeconomic framework.

Second, current asset pricing models seem deficient in explaining many of these return effects. The CAPM and various extensions thereof—zero beta, multifactor, and consumption-based CAPM—cannot fully explain anomalies. Recent research shows that the arbitrage pricing theory (APT) does little better. In fact, it is difficult to conceive of any meaningful definition of risk that is as transient as are some of the documented return effects. Furthermore, such fleeting effects should be immune to Roll's critique of CAPM, as they are likely robust to any reasonable definition of the market portfolio (Roll, 1977). Nevertheless progress is constantly being made on the theoretical front. For example, an article by Merton [1987] propounded an extension of CAPM with incomplete information that is consistent with neglected firm, small size, sigma, and many other effects.

Finally, disentangling is key for efficacious common stock management. Only by unraveling the various return effects can one hope to understand them, and only then can one hope to exploit them.

INVESTMENT STRATEGIES

Three investment strategies are consisted with the analysis set forth in this presentation. The first strategy is the anomaly capture strategy: It is akin to a multi-tilted indexing approach, although somewhat more elaborate. It is simple to understand and implement if you have a multi-anomaly model at your disposal. This approach involves placing bets on several anomalies simultaneously, where the strength of each bet would be a function of the historical strength and consistency of that anomaly. Further, because these anomalies are measured in pure form, they have the benefit of being fully additive. This strategy is particularly attractive to investors with a low risk tolerance.

There are several reasons why anomalies might be expected to persist. First, many have such long historical track records as to belie the argument that they are mere flukes. Second, investor psychology suggests the continued existence of some anomalies (Jacobs and Levy, 1987). Third, insitutional factors underlying some anomalies are quite rigid. Finally, as discussed earlier, there is emerging theoretical support for the existence of anomalies.

There are some drawbacks to this approach, however. First, it is empirically rather than analytically based. It is designed to fit the observed state of nature and skeptics might call it data mining. Second, some effects may be nonstationary. To the extent that anomalies are less than fully stationary, they will be harder to predict; the recent performance of size and P/E are examples. Also, it may omit pertinent information about the time variation in returns.

The second recommended strategy is time-series modeling. The strategy is designed to exploit the time patterns in anomaly returns using time-series techniques to model the stochastic processes underlying the return series. It has potentially greater rewards, but also potentially greater risks than the anomaly capture strategy. To the extent that the stochastic processes are not fully stationary, forecast errors will result. Also, turnover will be higher than for anomaly capture.

The third recommended strategy, the most dynamic and adaptive of all, is macroeconomic modeling. It presumes neither the persistent payoffs of anomaly capture nor the time-pattern stationarity of time-series modeling. Rather, it adopts a broader framework by incorporating macroeconomic drivers in its search for empirical return regularities. Further, it provides investment insight into the forces driving equity return; and it can be classified as full active management offering the allure of potential superior performance. On the other hand, its drawbacks include possible structural instability, which would decrease forecast accuracy, and increased complexity, requiring substantial expertise.

Investment Opportunities with Indexing

Jeffrey L. Skelton

Index funds have been a fixture of the investment management business for more than 17 years. Much of their extraordinary success may be attributed to their proven ability to deliver reliably close returns to "cost-free" market benchmarks. Curiously, the low-cost, highly-controlled investment processes that make indexing possible may also be employed in strategies that aim to beat the market averages.

INDEXING AND EFFICIENT MARKETS

The roots of indexing are in academia. In fact, the academic literature on efficient markets goes back farther than one might expect, to a turn-of-the-century study of the behavior of commodities prices in France (Bachelier, 1900). The study's startling finding was that commodities prices seemed to be a fair game—they were about as likely to go up as down. The intellectual thread was picked up in the late 1950s and early 1960s by a number of researchers who investigated the behavior of stock prices and reached similar, if somewhat more sophisticated, conclusions: that the distribution of stock market returns seemed to be constant over time.

At about the same time that evidence was mounting that demonstrated the random nature of securities prices, the investment management industry was beginning to measure itself against market benchmarks such as the S&P 500. The results for the industry were disappointing, to say the least. Active management was denounced by academics and some practitioners of the burgeoning index fund business as a bankrupt process.

In the mid-to-late 1970s, however, contradictions or anomalies began to appear in the academic literature on efficient markets. Some careful examinations of the return data for equities suggested that systematic factors or characteristics of securities might be "priced". That is, securities smaller than average, or higher-yielding than average, or less liquid than average might be underpriced relative to the market.

Why might such anomalies exist? Perhaps they exist because the assumptions leading to the intellectual conclusion that markets are efficient are simply too far from the practical truth. Information is not free, and capital does not necessarily move quickly and without cost to an opportunity. Rather, practical barriers may inhibit the flow of information and capital in ways that produce reliable profit opportunities for uninhibited investors.

Subtle, but important, barriers are erected by investment managers themselves. From portfolio construction to trading to portfolio monitoring, most managers are terribly inefficient processors of securities. The result is that managers who can control costs and risks more effectively may succeed where the majority do not. To do so, active managers must learn from indexers.

ACTIVE AND PASSIVE MANAGEMENT

Active and passive management styles may be compared along three dimensions: portfolio construction, trading and monitoring. Figure 1 illustrates the differences.

The typical active manager expends the majority of its resources on portfolio construction—the process of deciding which stocks to buy or sell. Analysts and portfolio managers pore over information and make subjective evaluations of the attractiveness of securities. Because the individuals qualified for such jobs are expensive, and because their thought processes are time-consuming, the resulting list of stocks for the portfolio is small—perhaps 20 to 50 names. By contrast, portfolio construction for passive managers is very simple. The desired securities are simply the stocks comprising the index. Equity indexes may contain 500 to 5,000 names.

Trading techniques in both styles of management are an expression of the need to accommodate the results of portfolio construction. In many actively-managed portfolios, the size of each stock position is large relative to the ability of the market to accommodate the desired trade. To minimize the effect of potentially large transactions, trades are "worked" or executed in

FIGURE 1. The Investment Management Process

Portfolio Construction

Active	Passive
Subjective	Objective
Complex Rules	Simple Rules
Few Names	Many Names
Approximate Weightings	Precise Weightings

Trading

Active	Passive
Worked Transactions	Program Transactions
Few Names	Many Names
Cash Reserves	Fully Vested

Monitoring

Active	Passive
Infrequent	Constant
Approximate	Detailed

Source: Wells Fargo Investment Advisors

small blocks over hours, days, or even weeks. Trade working is imprecise and difficult to control, however, and thus the active manager's buying and selling may not be well matched. To avoid buying more than has been sold, a modest amount of cash must be maintained in the portfolio.

Because the typical index fund has 10 to 100 times the number of securities in the typical active portfolio, and because securities are normally held in capitalization weight, the market impact of trades is not a problem. The challenge to passive managers is to execute an extraordinarily large number of transactions quickly, precisely, and at minimum cost. Most passive trading is in the form of packages or programs, in which hundreds or thousands of stocks are traded at one moment in time. The precision of program techniques allows index funds to be managed with virtually no cash reserves.

Perhaps because an active portfolio has subjective weightings for securities and is difficult to control, the monitoring of its structure is infrequent and imprecise. For exactly the opposite reasons, monitoring of the structure of indexed portfolios must be constant and as complete as possible.

Clearly, the byproduct of learning simply to replicate benchmarks has been to create an exceptionally efficient investment process. Passive managers may move more money across more securities with far greater precision and economy than active managers.

THE PAYOFF TO PASSIVE MANAGEMENT

The agility and precision of passive management styles may be exploited in strategies that profit from efficient and timely moves across broad asset classes. Three such strategies are index arbitrage, market tilting, and tactical asset allocation.

Index arbitrage is the opportunistic exchange of stocks with futures positions and cash. Evaluating an opportunity in the strategy is simple. Realizing the potential profits in the transaction is far more difficult. Every arbitrage transaction is actually 502 transactions—500 stocks, money market instruments, and futures. Only precise timing and the most efficient execution can assure successful arbitrage. Not surprisingly, most arbitrage strategies are managed by indexers.

Market-tilt strategies exploit systematic pricing differences or anomalies in equity markets. Size, tax, and value characteristics are carefully engineered in very broadly diversified portfolios. Market-tilt portfolios may contain 500 to 1,000 securities held in precisely determined weights. Program-trading techniques are used to minimize cash balances and ensure efficient implementation of trade lists. Again, not surprisingly, most market-tilt strategies are managed by indexers.

Tactical asset allocation (TAA) is a conceptually simple evaluation of value across stocks, bonds, and cash with proportions in each determined by portfolio optimization.

As with other passive-related strategies, TAA's portfolio construction process is objective. As such, it is unimpaired by bureaucratic barriers to changes in asset mixes and by emotional responses to market behavior. Implementation of mix recommendations with index funds assures that a given market's attractive relative value is captured. Passive trading techniques assure that mix changes occur quickly and at lowest cost. As with arbitrage and market tilting, most TAA strategies are managed by indexers.

THE FUTURE OF THE INVESTMENT MANAGEMENT BUSINESS

An investment manager's product is the result produced in the client's portfolio. As with any product, reliability and economy are important characteristics to the buyer. The technique passive managers use to produce low-cost, highly-controlled investment outcomes must eventually be adopted throughout the industry. Otherwise, active managers will continue to produce disappointing results, and, like other dinosaurs, disappear from the scene.

Question and Answer Session

QUESTION: Why did you begin your analysis in 1978?

JACOBS: Our analysis covers nine years; this is sufficient to reveal many effects which have substantial *t*-statistics, such as the residual reversal effect. Also, some of the measures that we have utilized, such as those based on expectational data, were not available earlier. The problem with trying to use more years is that many attributes will have incomplete or missing data. We preferred to have a more complete model, representing 1,500 stocks over a shorter time span, rather than a longer time span with less complete data.

QUESTION: Did you test for nonlinear or combined factors?

LEVY: We tested for linearity in all of the measures, and in fact a lot of them are not linear. The U-shaped yield curve is one example. As another example, the size effect is not linear in firm capitalization, but is linear in the log of capitalization.

JACOBS: Most multifactor risk modelling utilizes factors which are composites of attributes. As you can see, our approach is very different. We believe in fully disentangling all attributes to measure the various cross-currents in the marketplace, and that this is a very effective design for money management.

QUESTION: Have you controlled for market impact costs and transaction costs?

LEVY: The bid-ask spread was a concern. In the historical analysis, we lagged price one month to alleviate this concern. For example, market capitalization was calculated using shares outstanding at time t and prices at time t-1. This gets around the problem of capturing pricing errors or bid-ask spreads. One of our measures is low price, so if a bid-ask spread is picked up by that measure, the other anomalies would be immune to that criticism. One could argue that if we had not lagged price, the low price measure would suffer from that defect.

JACOBS: One might argue that the payoffs to our measures reflect average transaction costs because we include both price and market capitalization. Price, on a percentage basis, takes into account commissions; on the other hand, the market capitalization measure represents potential market impact costs. So one might say that the payoffs to each of our measures is a payoff to an average market capitalization and an average price, reflecting an average commission and an average market impact. Yet, there is still a payoff associated with it.

QUESTION: Why has the Wells Fargo asset allocation model done so poorly in 1987 through September?

SKELTON: The spread in expected return between stocks and bonds is at a historic low; that is, the stock market seems to be overvalued relative to the bond market. Wells Fargo's strategies are heavily invested in bonds at the moment. We fully expect a convergence to fair value. In asset allocation, unlike arbitrage, convergence is not guaranteed.

QUESTION: What was the performance of the Wells Fargo tilt portfolios over the past 12 months?

SKELTON: Over the past 12 months, the tilt portfolios have been about even. To be fair, the tilt strategies have had a disappointing 1987. All the stocks that seemed to be undervalued simply became more undervalued during 1987.

Security Analysis, DDMs, and Probability

H. Russell Fogler

In this presentation, I would like to address three questions. First, is security analysis related to probability distributions? Second, can security analysis be incorporated into dividend discount models (DDMs)? And third, will multifactor models replace dividend discount models?

SECURITY ANALYSIS, PROBABILITY, SKEWNESS, AND EXCESS RETURNS

To answer the question of whether security analysis is related to probability distributions, I looked at the relative returns—i.e., after subtracting the S&P 500—of a portfolio of stocks. Table 1 lists the 20 best and the 20 worst stocks in the Aronson and Fogler portfolio based on their relative performance for 1986. Because the best returns are consistently higher than the worst returns, the portfolio's distribution is said to be "positively skewed." In fact, actual results would have been more skewed because several of the worst stocks were eliminated when they began to decline.

The goal of security analysis is to get rid of the bottom tail of the distribution. By dropping the largest losers, the mean of the distribution moves up. It is a very simple mathematical law. Figure 1 presents the normal distribution, high-lighting the goal of security analysts to eliminate the tail of the distribution. If the market is truly mean-variance efficient, then dropping the bottom of the tail improves mean-variance efficiency—and performance. Few, if any, distributions would be so left-skewed that they could have a higher mean without having a higher variance. Thus, at any given variance level, a positively skewed distribution has a higher return. This is illustrated in Figure 2.[1]

COMBINING SECURITY ANALYSIS AND DDMs

In chapter 3 of Brown and Kritzman's *Quantitative Methods for Financial Analysis*, I demonstrate the application of quantitative methods to equity analysis. The following comments on valuation are drawn from that discussion.

Table 2 contains present value and dividend discount model (DDM) calculations for ABC in 1985, before it was taken over by Capital Cities.

FIGURE 1. Mean/Variance Efficiency Helps: Downside is Cut Off

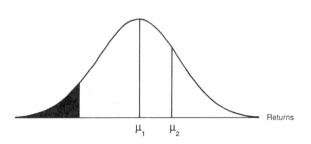

μ₁ μ₂ Returns

Source: Aronson + Fogler

FIGURE 2. Mean/Variance Efficiency Helps: Same Variance Requires Same Mean

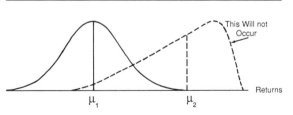

This Will not Occur

μ₁ μ₂ Returns

Source: Aronson + Fogler

[1] Although there is considerable evidence that simple mean-variance efficiency is an adequate description of the risk/return relation, Arditti (1967) provided a strong argument that positive skewness should be priced. Whether skewness is actually priced is still open to question; Peterson and Peterson (1982) supply some empirical results. A more general theoretical statement is provided in Kraus and Litzenberger (1983).

Best Returns		Worst Returns	
Fuji Photo	108.38%	Redken Labs	−34.43%
Robertshaw Ctls.	100.85	Texas Inds.	−35.34
Matsushita Elec.	79.41	Comdisco Inc.	−35.36
Russell Corp.	65.02	Moore McCormack	−35.56
Savannah Elec. & Pwr.	62.77	Amrep Corp.	−36.28
Medtronic Inc.	60.52	Honeywell Inc.	−36.58
Chesebrough Ponds	58.67	Grumman Corp.	−38.06
Tyco Labs Inc.	56.40	Fluke John Mfg.	−38.19
Standard Pac. Corp.	55.23	Burlington Northern	−38.40
AFG Inds. Inc.	54.55	Golden Nugget Inc.	−38.97
Monfort Colo. Inc.	52.86	Savannah Foods	−39.94
Collins & Aikman	51.60	Bell Inds.	−40.02
American Bakeries	48.13	Cubic Corp.	−44.90
Ex Cell O Corp.	46.76	Teradyne Inc.	−47.73
Celanese Corp.	45.00	Southdown Inc.	−48.67
Alexander & Baldwin	44.84	United Indl.	−50.80
RJR Nabisco Inc.	43.91	Farah Mfg. Inc.	−51.28
Royal Dutch Petroleum	42.30	Radice Corp.	−55.29
Unifi Inc.	42.08	Allegheny Beverage	−83.85
Shell Trans. & Trad.	41.97	First City Bancorp	−92.10
	56.44%		−45.91%

Source: Aronson + Fogler

Unfortunately, the simple DDM calculation indicates a present value of only $53.88, below the market price of $64 and well below the $121 that Capital Cities eventually paid!

The basic calculations in Table 2 are as follows. Using a simple constant growth dividend discount model, and the assumption that dividends and earnings would grow 10 percent per year, the 1989 value of ABC is $85.67 per share, at a capitalization rate of 13 percent. Imputing this 1989 value with five years of projected dividends, the 1985 present value is estimated as $53.88. This price is below the market price of $64 in January 1985. A price earnings DDM yields a similar result. Thus,

simple DDM models suggested that the market was overpricing ABC stock. Of course, hindsight would lead one to a different conclusion as the stock doubled in value.

The question is: How does one find companies like ABC, whose stock price doubles? Could either quantitative methods or security analysis help? I think the answer is 'yes,' and I use the phrase "DDMs with Micro-Probabilities" to explain how.

The ABC example may be expanded to illustrate my point. In 1980, ABC had $220 million in debt. That year, and later, interest rates rose to more than 13 percent. ABC's management probably reasoned that it should not float new debt; they reduced their debt by $80 million, down to $140 million in debt over four years. At the same time, by retaining earnings, they increased their equity substantially.

At this point, a little security analysis helps. Potential DDM modellers might have asked whether ABC was really producing only $1.60 in dividends a year, and whether the dividends were going to grow at only 10 percent? Different assumptions were probably appropriate. Instead of assuming $1.60 in dividends, the dividend projection could easily have been increased to $2.15. After all, ABC was reducing

---

TABLE 2.   DDM Valuations: An Example

ABC: January-June 1985
Assumptions
1984 Dividend ($1.60) grows at 10%

$$PV = \frac{D}{r-g}$$

$$P_{1989} = \frac{2.57}{.13 - .10} = \$85.67$$

$$PV = \frac{1.75}{1.13} + \frac{1.94}{1.28} + \frac{2.13}{1.44} + \frac{2.34}{1.63} + \frac{2.57}{1.84} + \frac{85.67}{1.84} = \$53.88$$

Source: Stephen J. Brown and Mark P. Kritzman, eds. *Quantitative Methods for Financial Analysis.* (Homewood IL: Dow Jones-Irwin, 1987).

Six Scenarios	DDM Value
1. $D_0 = \$1.60$, $P_5 = \$85.67$	$53.88
2. $D_0 = \$2.15$, $P_5 = \$105.00$	66.01
3. $D_0 = \$2.15$, $P_5 = \$115.41$	71.76
4. Scenario #1 plus $5	58.88
5. Scenario #2 plus $5	71.01
6. Scenario #3 plus $5	76.76

TABLE 3. DDMs and Security Analysis

Source: Stephen J. Brown and Mark P. Kritzman, eds. *Quantitative Methods for Financial Analysis.* (Homewood IL: Dow Jones-Irwin, 1987).

their debt by about $20 million per year. This money could have been used to pay dividends instead.

Table 3 presents two prices based on a $2.15 dividend. The second calculation—scenario 3—is higher because it assumes that earnings would continue to grow at 10 percent even though ABC was not plowing back as much earnings (for a more complete explanation, see Brown and Kritzman, 1987, chapter 3). Now there are three prices: $54 if the original dividend assumption is used; $66 if the dividend is increased to $2.15, which seemed like no burden; and $72 if the earnings continue to grow at 10 percent and the higher dividend is used.

Additionally, a new owner could borrow $150 million and still have the same capital structure that ABC had in 1980. That translates into another $5 per share. In Table 3, scenarios 4, 5, and 6 incorporate the additional $5 per share value. Accordingly, the DDM value increases to as much as $77 per share.

Unfortunately, there are now six values, but only one DDM. One way to resolve this dilemma is to use probability analysis. Each scenario may be assigned a probability, and the mean value may be calculated. Figure 3 illustrates this process.

In Figure 3, the average price is $67 versus a $64 current market price, and the "skewness odds" are very favorable. Although it would be hard to say whether the stock was worth buying for a difference of $3, the odds of loss, or downside risk, is only 20 percent. Clearly, the upside potential was much better than the downside risk—the odds were about 4 to 1, in a sense. This is a skewed probability distribution, and the function of security analysis is to try to

skew the distribution in your favor.[2] Certainly, DDM projections may be more powerful and realistic by incorporating information from security analysis.

WILL MULTIFACTOR MODELS DISPLACE DDMs?

Despite the usefulness of probabilistic DDMs, they may not always be appropriate. There are four reasons for using factor models: (1) factor models seem to work well; (2) there is a time horizon problem with DDMs; (3) DDMs are sensitive to assumed rates of growth or capitalization; and (4) DDMs do not explicitly consider factor diversification.

The real impetus for multifactor models is that they have worked in the past. I would

FIGURE 3. How Security Analysis Might Skew Selection

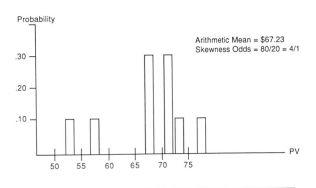

Source: Stephen J. Brown and Mark P. Kritzman, eds. *Quantitative Methods for Financial Analysis.* (Homewood IL: Dow Jones-Irwin, 1987).

suggest that some factor models are going to work in the future, as well. Risk is the major reason that they work. Single-A-rated bonds typically have a higher return over a 10-year period than government bonds, because they are riskier. Similarly, small firms will probably have higher returns than large firms over a

[2] I do not mean "skewed" in the sense of looking at past return distributions for the stock, because those evaporate when you try to carry them into the future with a large portfolio. Conine and Tamerkin (1981) demonstrate this effect.

FIGURE 4. Multifactor Diversification

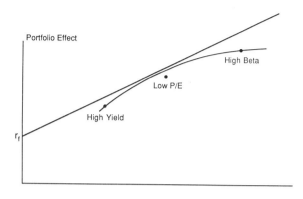

Source: Aronson + Fogler

FIGURE 5. Enhanced Performance through Factor Models

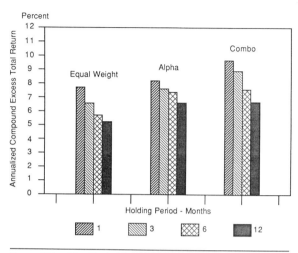

Source: Columbine Capital Services

10-year period because they tend to be riskier. Consequently, the past success of the size factor is easily explainable. A paper by Fielitz and Muller (1985) showed that dividend discount models do very well; but the same results were obtained using naive factor models.

The second reason is the time horizon problem. Dividend discount models produce different rates of return if the explicit time horizon is changed (the exception is when the assumed growth rate equals the capitalization rate from now till the horizon). Thus, "early" takeovers will produce different rates than longer forecasts.

Sensitivity to rates of return is the third problem with DDMs. There is a great deal of sensitivity to the numbers in dividend discount models. The estimated value can double when one moves from a capitalization rate of 14 to 12 percent. In the ABC example, if the 1989 price were estimated using a capitalization rate of 14 percent, the value would be $64.25 [2.15/(.14 − .10)]; but, if the rate was 12 percent, the value would be $128.50 [2.15/(.12 − .10)]. This is less of a problem if relative values are used for comparisons.

The fourth limitation of DDMs is their failure to provide explicit diversification. For example, assume that a multifactor model is created weighted in three factors: beta, high growth, and low P/E. If the returns from these factors are not perfectly correlated, then the factors contribute their own diversifications. Intuitively, each factor is like a portfolio of stocks that weight heavily on that factor, and combinations of those factor portfolios produce a better diversi-

fied risk/return frontier. This is an extension of the Markowitz efficient frontier concept. Figure 4 illustrates the efficient frontier with the factors.

The powerful effect of multifactor diversification causes better performance. Figure 5 shows tests for three models over four holding periods: one, three, six, and twelve months. The equal-weight model selected stocks based on the fundamental criteria. The Alpha II model is based on price data. Individually, the models return approximately 8 percent. But when these models are combined in a multifactor model ("Combo"), the returns increased by 2 percent. Simply put, better performance is *always* achieved if there is multifactor diversification; it results from rebalancing—by selling the better performing factor stocks and buying the poor performing factor stocks.

Will the inherent diversification advantages cause multifactor models to replace DDMs? Hardly. Diversification is not enough, and return-oriented models are needed.

CONCLUSION

In closing, one more factor should be mentioned: the human factor. Better models are built upon human thought and analysis. The market is highly efficient, especially if returns for human capital are subtracted from raw returns. Better valuation models will assist us in using our minds more effectively.

Future quantitative models will combine security analysis, probablility, and cashflow discounting. In addition to the "micro" probabilities discussed above, "macro" probabilities will extend the distributional richness for events such as unanticipated inflations, recessions, and bear markets. Further, by constructing portfolios with an optimizer, securities with the highest DDM return forecasts will be combined in a portfolio that is diversified by factors.

Valuation Models for Equity Securities

Preston W. Estep

Security analysts seem to spend a great deal of time thinking about things other than expected return. They think about whether the management is good, whether the products are proprietary, whether the company faces foreign competition, and whether the inventories have been rising or falling. They use this information to make financial forecasts. In truth, the only thing that analysts should care about is how to find stocks that will exhibit superior returns. I would like to discuss how we may take these analysts' forecasts and turn them into forecasts of expected return which have nothing to do with historical attributes, regression models, or other data-searching techniques.

Let us begin with a definition of return. Total return is the summation of the cashflows received and the price changes received. Return may be rewritten in terms of growth, cashflow yield, and valuation change, as illustrated in Figure 1. This equation is known as the T-model. In the model, g stands for the growth in book value; PB stands for the price/book ratio; and $\triangle$PB is the change in the price/book ratio. (For example, if the price/book ratio went from 2.0 to 2.1, $\triangle$PB would be 0.1.) The T-model is not conjectural; for a given set of data, the model derives the exact total return for the period.

In this model, cashflows are not simply equal to dividend over price because the company may repurchase or issue shares during the year, which is another way of getting cash to shareholders. To illustrate this point, imagine that you own a company that will invest in plant and equipment to the extent required, and will pay the excess capital to the owner either as a dividend, or by repurchasing shares. If the company needs to invest more in plant and equipment than it generated in earnings, it will issue additional shares and some debt to raise the money, keeping its capital structure the same. Under these circumstances, dividends plus the share transactions equal return on equity (ROE) minus growth (g) over the price/book ratio—the middle term in the T-model.

Return on equity is equal to the company's earnings divided by its book value. These three terms are not factors; they are things that the company does. In real life this is not perfectly true, because the company's capital structure does not actually stay the same, as assumed above.

To verify that the T-model is a correct representation of return in terms of financial variables, reported financial data can be used as inputs and the resulting estimated return compared with actual return. Table 1 shows 1985 financial data for IBM. In 1985, IBM's growth was 20.8 percent; the change in the price/book ratio was 5.0; and the return on equity was 24.7 percent. Based on this data, a shareholder of IBM should have received a return of 28.3 percent, as illustrated in Table 1. Actually, the return that year was 29.9 percent. The difference can be explained by the fact that IBM should have issued some shares according to this model, but did not; their debt/equity ratio rose slightly that year.

Table 2 shows the same calculation for the 30 stocks in the Dow Jones Industrial Average. There is a close correspondence between the returns estimated with this model and actual returns. I am not claiming that this is a fitted

---

FIGURE 1. The T-Model Valuation Formula

$$T = g + \frac{ROE - g}{PB} + \frac{\triangle PB}{PB}(1 + g),$$

where:

T = total return in the period
g = growth of shareholders' equity over the period,
ROE = net income in the period divided by beginning shareholders' equity
PB = beginning aggregate market value of firm's common stock divided by beginning shareholders' equity, and
$\triangle$PB = change in PB, or PB at end of period − PB at beginning of period.

Source: New Amsterdam Partners

TABLE 1. 1985 Financial Data for IBM

Net Income	$ 6,555 mil.
Dividends Paid	$ 2,703 mil.
Beginning Equity	$26,489 mil.
Ending Equity	$31,990 mil.
Change in Equity	20.8%
Return on Beginning Equity	24.7%
Dividend Yield	3.59%
Beginning Shares Out	612.9 mil.
Ending Shares Out	615.4 mil.
Change in Shares Out	0.41%
Price at Beginning of Year	$ 123.125
Price at End of Year	$ 155.5
Price/Book at Beginning	2.85
Price/Book at End	2.99
Change in Price/Book	5.0%
T-Model Results:	
Growth of Equity	20.8%
CashFlow Yield	1.4%
Valuation Change	6.1%
Estimated Return	28.3%
Actual Return	29.9%

Source: New Amsterdam Partners

TABLE 2. Sources of Return for the 30 Dow Jones Stocks in 1985

Stock Ticker Symbol	Growth of Equity + (g)	Cash-Flow Yield + $\left(\frac{ROE-g}{PB}\right)$	Valuation Change = $\left(\frac{\Delta PB}{PB}\right)(1+g)$	Est. Return (T)	Actual Return
UK	−18.4%	12.5%	103.5%	97.6%	102.0%
WX	−13.5	24.3	63.4	74.2	74.7
ALD	112.3	−117.5	73.6	68.5	42.4
Z	16.4	0.4	48.7	65.6	67.7
MCD	12.6	4.2	41.0	57.7	58.3
MRK	3.5	6.6	38.3	48.5	49.2
AXP	15.7	1.5	28.6	45.8	44.4
DD	3.6	5.8	34.2	43.5	43.2
T	6.3	3.4	25.8	35.5	34.5
OI	9.7	1.5	23.6	34.8	35.4
GE	10.6	3.9	18.2	32.7	32.4
CHV	5.4	7.1	16.6	29.1	29.7
IBM	20.8	1.4	6.1	28.3	29.9
XON	0.8	13.1	13.5	27.5	29.9
PG	3.8	4.7	18.9	27.3	26.9
S	8.3	3.7	15.4	27.3	28.4
AC	21.0	−5.8	11.9	27.1	24.8
GT	10.6	2.8	11.4	24.8	26.4
UTX	5.6	2.5	16.6	24.7	24.6
MMM	5.1	5.1	7.4	17.6	18.6
MO	15.7	6.2	−8.0	14.0	14.5
X	11.2	−4.8	6.2	12.5	6.3
EK	−8.1	8.1	10.2	10.3	10.6
N	8.0	−1.7	3.4	9.7	8.7
AA	−1.1	0.6	5.4	5.0	7.3
IP	−3.1	8.8	−6.5	−0.9	−1.4
TX	4.0	8.8	−15.6	−2.8	−3.3
BS	−15.6	−6.2	15.3	−6.5	−8.9
NAV	39.7	24.6	−25.7	−10.7	4.6
GM	22.2	−5.3	−32.2	−15.3	−3.7

Source: New Amsterdam Partners

model; this is simply plugging hindsight into a mathematical identity. But the fit between estimated and actual return is very good (R-squared of 0.94). Note: For statistical models, even when all the data is known by perfect hindsight, the typical cross-sectional R-squared is only about 0.10.

FORECASTING INPUTS

Russ Fogler's discussion on making forecasts and the need to clean them up made a lot of sense.[1] But, suppose an analyst went through that exercise 50 times and determined that each company was fairly valued. He would have wasted a great deal of time, and still would not have anything to invest in. An alternative would be to approach the analysis in an algorithmic way. The most rational way to seek high return seems to be to forecast it directly through its three components: ROE, growth, and the changes in the price/book ratio. The details on forecasting are beyond the scope of this presentation; however, my recent article in the *Financial Analysts Journal* provides some guidelines (Estep, 1987).

The T-Model generates accurate forecasts if the input numbers are known. If the numbers

[1] See Dr. Fogler's presentation, pp. 51–55.

must be estimated, then the model is less precise. I would like to demonstrate how to plug estimated numbers into this model and try to guess which stocks will be good and which will be bad.

Table 3 shows a comparison of the T-model for Baxter Labs and C. R. Bard. The data required as input to the model may be obtained in database or machine-readable form from most brokerage firms. The example also assumes that both of these companies would some day sell at twice book value ($\Delta PB=2$). At the time this table was compiled, most Wall Street analysts were recommending Baxter, although it is not clear why. The growth rate was lower, the P/E was higher, and the ROE was lower. According to the T-model, the expected return for Bard was 12.7 percent; for Baxter, it was 9.3 percent. This

TABLE 3. T-Model Comparison

	Baxter Labs	C. R. Bard*
Price ($)	19.25	24.75
Earnings per share ($)	0.88	1.57
Book/Share	5.35	8.25
Growth Rate (%)	10.0	12.3
ROE (%)	16.4	19.0
PB	3.6	3.0
ΔPB	2.0	2.0
n	20	20
Total Return (%)	9.3%	12.7%

* Data adjusted for subsequent two-for-one split.
Source: New Amsterdam Partners

would suggest buying Bard and selling Baxter. Actually, one should do some further sensitivity analysis to see whether the numbers are robust, but this example shows how to use the T-model to get estimates of the expected return on a particular company.

The T-model is an equation for return in terms of fundamentals. It is an analytical model, and, as such, it can be used to figure out some of the so-called market-efficiency anomalies. The model can be used to answer the question: What is the so called price/book effect that makes stocks with low price/book ratios have higher returns? What is the price/earnings effect that makes stocks with low P/E ratios have higher returns? These representations of expected return result from applying simplifying assumptions in the T-Model. For example, if growth is assumed to be zero, and price/book is constant; or if price/book is always one, the expected return is equal to earnings over price (E/P), and the stock's expected return would also equal E/P. So, when someone uses E/P to predict expected return, that only indicates that they are not trying to forecast growth rates. The P/E effect is a test of two assumptions: That growth is the same (zero) for all stocks, and that price/book does not change much. I suppose that it is an anomaly that those two assumptions have not been arbitraged away.

Similarly, the price/book effect can also be explained. We see that PB appears in the denominator, and that low price/book usually raises return, especially if we assume that price/book reverts to some mean. This assumption turns out to be true more often than not. But these are empirical issues. It is perfectly possible to have a market in which the participants make good growth forecasts, and price/

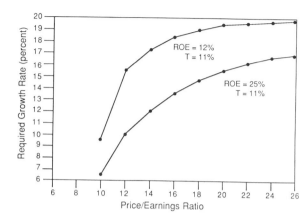

FIGURE 2. The Price of Growth Depends on ROE

Source: New Amsterdam Partners

book does not revert to a mean. The T-Model would still be as true as ever, but the P/E effect and price/book effect would not be observed.

Another familiar formula is that expected return equals yield plus growth—Gordon-Shapiro's simplified version of the dividend discount model. That is true when growth exactly equals the reinvestment rate, and the price/book ratio stays constant.

Bob Hagin mentioned that ROE is perverse; that is, if you buy stocks with high ROEs, you get worse returns.[2] That is interesting. The T-model has ROE in the numerator of the second term. If everything else was equal, raising the ROE must raise the return. But everything else is not equal, because people overprice rising ROE stocks. For some reason, people like ROE more than they ought to; so high-ROE stocks tend to diminish in value and low ROE stocks tend to go up. Empirical research will readily verify that both things are true.

The relationship between growth, ROE, and the price/earnings ratio is important. Figure 2 illustrates how the price of growth depends on ROE. The required growth rate is on the vertical axis, and the P/E is on the horizontal axis. Therefore, if the ROE is 25 percent and an investor only wanted an expected return of 11 percent, then he would pay 14 times earnings for a company growing at 12 percent. If, however, the ROE was only 12 percent, the company would have to be growing at 18 percent for someone to pay 14 times earnings. Note that

---

[2] See Dr. Hagin's presentation, pp. 16–20.

those relationships are dependent on expected return. A different expected return would produce a different family of curves.

Similarly, there is a trade-off between growth and ROE. If the growth rate is held constant, it seems plausible that companies with higher ROEs are worth more—as illustrated in Figure 3. For example, if a company is growing at 8 percent, and an investor wanted an expected return of 11 percent; that investor would pay 8 times earnings if the ROE was 16 percent; but only pay 14 times earnings if the ROE was 30 percent. If the growth rate is 18 percent, however, the investor might pay very high P/Es for much lower returns on equity. Also, as I mentioned earlier, these relationships depend on the level of the required return. As the stock market goes up and down, the average expected return of all the stocks goes with it. That is, as the Dow Jones Industrial Average went from 1500 to 2500, the average expected return on its stocks, according to my estimates, declined from about 13 percent to about 10.5 percent.

Thus, the relationship among P/Es in the market will change in a way that can be determined analytically. For a company with a return on equity of 25 percent, and a 13.5 percent growth rate, the price/earnings ratio should be 16 if one's required rate of return is 11 percent, as Figure 3 illustrates. If, however, someone wanted an expected return of 16 percent, then he would not pay that much, unless the company was growing at 21 percent. So there is a pronounced difference in valuation relationships as the market and the average expected returns go up and down. This causes all sorts of bizarre cross-currents in industry group valuations as well as in P/E quintile valuations.

In conclusion, I will briefly address the subject of regression. In *Cybernetics*, one of the most influential books of the 20th century, Nor-

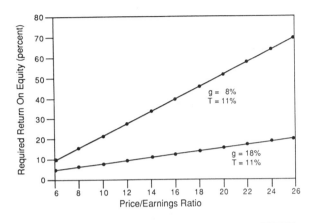

FIGURE 3. At a Given Growth Rate, Higher ROE is Worth a Higher Price

Source: New Amsterdam Partners

bert Weiner explored the future of analyzing all sorts of things with computers and multiple regression techniques (Weiner 1948). He was also a very important pioneer—and an early critic—of statistical methods of social sciences, and he said the following: "The psychology of the fools becomes a subject well worth the serious attention of the knave. There are always statisticians, sociologists, and economists ready to sell their services to these undertakings. These techniques can never furnish us with a quantity of verifiable significant information which begins to compare with that which we have learned to expect in the natural sciences." Gunter Murdough similarly said, "Correlations are not explanations and can be spurious, as, for example, the high correlation in Finland between foxes killed and divorce." In the final analysis, however, Dr. Weiner was just a pessimist. He is the man who said that the natural stable state of a living organism is death.

Equity Duration

Eric H. Sorensen

The topic of equity duration is still unfamiliar to many people. A simple survey would probably indicate that most people think of bonds when they hear the word duration; considerably fewer would think of equities or stocks. Nevertheless, equity duration is becoming more important in the real world, particularly among plan sponsors. I have two goals for this presentation: to identify what is meant by stock duration, and to prove that it is important.

There are at least three ways to think about duration. First, duration may be thought of as a measure of the time-weighted receipt of principal and interest cash flows. This concept goes back to Hicks and Macaulay's classic articles of the late 1930s (Hicks, 1939 and Macaulay, 1938). They wrote their articles separately, but came to the same conclusion: that one way to think about a financial asset is to assess its sensitivity or response to changes in interest rates. They actually calculated a formula, which is the present-value weighted time to the receipt of principal and income of that financial asset. This leads to the second way of thinking about duration. If one makes some simplifying assumptions about how interest rates change, duration may be thought of as the derivative of the valuation formula—the dividend discount model (DDM), for example. The third way of thinking about duration is in terms of the concept of volatility. One characteristic of duration is that as the discount rate rises, the value of the asset has to fall, because the discount rate is in the denominator. Thus, duration is a measure of the sensitivity of the price of an asset to a change in interest rates. That has been the most common way to think of stock duration for the past five or ten years. With this perspective, one can measure the elasticity using time-series empirical techniques.

Each of these methods for calculating duration is legitimate; but each method generates a different answer. Is this a paradox? Does this mean that duration is a meaningless concept for equities, because we cannot agree on how to formulate and measure it?

DURATION: AN IMPORTANT FACTOR

There are two basic reasons why the concept of stock duration is important. First, stock duration may be used to assess the risk or volatility of the asset. In the context of the capital asset pricing model, beta is the measure of risk. There are also multifactor risk models—in simple terms, beta risk is captured in a number of specific attributes of securities, one of which might be a duration factor. If stocks have long durations because they are more sensitive to changes in interest rates, then the concept of stock duration is important—particularly in periods when interest rates are changing rapidly and volatility is increasing. Second, the equity market risk premium may be changing. It is elusive and hard to measure, but as it changes, the DDM duration formula will change. That is also something to consider for asset risk.

There seems to be an increasing interest in equity duration among financial analysts—plan sponsors, in particular. In the global sense, plan sponsors should be concerned with the management of the pension surplus—the excess of pension assets over the net present value of the pension liability—not just the assets (see Leibowitz, 1986). This concept has become more than a concept; it has become a point of interest because Statement of Financial Accounting Standards No. 87 (FAS 87) has forced plan sponsors to report any deficits in their pension fund surplus in their financial statements. Thus, plan sponsors are beginning to worry about their surplus exposure.

Analyzing a plan sponsor's exposure to the debt market is fairly straightforward, and it can be compared with the risk of the value of the liabilities. But many people also want exposure to equities, and it is not clear how to evaluate equity and debt on the same basis. It would be nice to have a summary risk measure which incorporates not only stock risk but also bond risk. Equity duration may be a solution.

Capital market theory identifies two sources of risk: systematic risk and nonsystematic risk.

<figure>

FIGURE 1. Duration for Stocks vs. Bonds

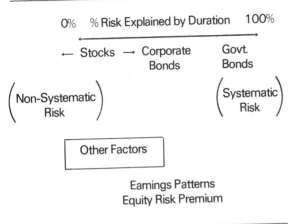

Source: Eric H. Sorensen

</figure>

These are diagrammed in Figure 1. Systematic risk is largely explained by macroeconomic variables. In finance theory, the market is the systematic risk for equities. In the bond market, interest rates determine the systematic risk. For global-asset-allocated portfolios, it may be some global benchmark. Most of us would agree that a major portion of the return to bonds is explained by systematic forces, and that considerably less equity return is explained by systematic risk. Nevertheless, the existence of indexing and other passive management strategies indicates that people are managing equities as if there is a systematic force out there.

Duration explains the risk of some securities better than others. Figure 1 illustrates the duration continuum from government bonds to equity. As one moves across the continuum, the percentage of risk explained by duration changes. Duration explains less risk for corporate bonds than government bonds; there may be call provisions, sinking funds, higher default risk, and so forth, so that duration is not the only factor. Stocks are at the extreme left of the continuum. Duration may help explain some of the volatility of the stock's price, but much of the movement in a stock's price may be nonsystematic relative to duration.

MODELING DURATION

Two factors must be considered in the development of an analytical model to deal with the concept of stock duration. First, the sources of risk that affect the value of the portfolio must be considered because risk affects the discount rate. Second, one must identify the stocks that are more sensitive to the factors influencing discount rate changes.

There are three key determinants of the relative duration between stocks: The stock's growth characteristics; the stock's discount rate, which is a function of risk; and the interaction between the discount rate and the growth assumptions. Figure 2 is a schematic that shows some of the interactive effects. Macroeconomic shocks affect the duration calculation in several ways. For example, a change in interest rates causes a response in the bond market, typically resulting in lower return on equities in the stock market. In a pure dividend discount model duration world, as rates rise and the discount rate goes up, the price of the asset falls. It has been argued that the sensitivity is 20 to 40 percent (a duration of 20 to 40 years)—that is, for a 100 basis point rise in interest rates, one would expect a 20 to 40 percent relative change in the price of the stock.

Inflationary expectations affect at least two variables in the valuation framework. First, changes in inflationary expectations may affect corporate revenue and profitability, which will ultimately have an impact on the stock price. If inflation causes changes in interest rates, it may also cause an acceleration in nominal economic activity. This is called a flow-through concept. Second, changes in inflationary expectations may affect the risk premium in the equity market. It is not clear how this would affect stock duration: it could make a duration higher or lower.

<figure>

FIGURE 2. Economic Transmission Scenario

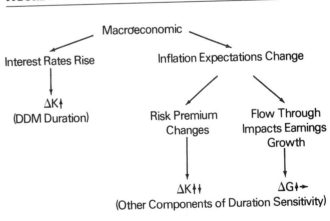

Source: Eric H. Sorensen

</figure>

Figure 3 illustrates the price movement of the S&P 500 versus the rate on long-term government bonds from 1960 to 1987. There is a long-term pattern of rising interest rates and rising stock prices between 1960 and 1987. This is not the intuitive pattern. Based on this figure, one might conclude that duration does not mean anything for a stock. In a shorter interval, however, there is a far more interesting relationship between the two lines. In 1969, there was a dramatic acceleration in interest rates and the stock market went down. That pattern occurred again in 1974, and again in 1981 and 1982. Based on these patterns, one could decide to avoid positions in the stock market during times when rates are going up. These are periods where stock duration is most extreme.

FIGURE 3. S&P 500 Price

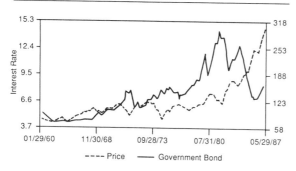

Source: Eric H. Sorensen

Figure 4 adds a line to the graph, and helps explain the stock market/interest rate interaction. The bond line is the same, though the scale is different; price has been decomposed into the S&P 500 P/E ratio and a proxy for profits (a measure of corporate profitability based on a government statistic). This figure helps to illustrate why the stock market was behaving strangely relative to interest rates during the 1960s, as shown in Figure 3; both the market and interest rates were rising and corporate profitability was doing very well. The stock market benefited from profitability throughout most of the 1970s. Figure 5 presents the S&P 500 P/E ratio versus the government bond interest rate over a slightly shorter time frame: 1970-87. Over the past 10 to 15 years, there has been a strong relationship between interest rates and stock market P/E ratios. This "visual analysis" is a throwback to Beryl Sprinkel. His book, *Money*

FIGURE 4. S&P 500 P/E and Corporate Profits

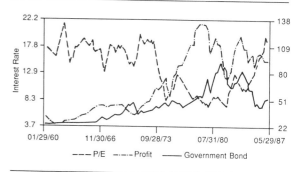

Source: Eric H. Sorensen

and Stock Prices (1964), included a graphic representation of the stock market and money supply. He pointed out that the stock market follows money supply, so that one may use money supply as an indicator to buy and sell stocks. Since that time, statistical techniques have been developed to measure those kinds of relationships, and it seems that our eye is not quite as good as a computer in analyzing patterns. One must be careful of computers, however. It is possible to draw very different conclusions depending on the statistical technique and the time period used.

The formula for dividend discount model duration has been worked out by a number of people (Boquist, Racette, and Schlarbaum, 1975). The formulation of DDM duration in Figure 6 makes two assumptions: (1) that the assumptions for the Gordon-Shapiro Constant Growth Model are applicable, and (2) price is equal to the present value of a dividend, compounded at rate *g*, which is a constant. After some mathematical manipulation, a simple

FIGURE 5. S&P 500 P/E

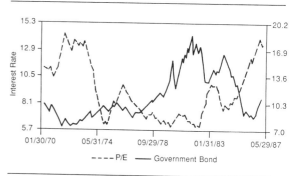

Source: Eric H. Sorensen

FIGURE 6. Derivation of DDM Duration

$$P = \sum_{t}^{\infty} \frac{D_t}{(1+k)^t}$$

$$P = \sum_{t}^{\infty} \frac{D_o (1+g)^t}{(1+k)^t}$$

$$P = \frac{D_o (1+g)}{k-g}$$

$$D_{DDM} = \frac{\partial \ln P}{\partial k} = \frac{1}{k-g}$$

where:

P = theoretical value of the stock
D_t = dividend at end of period t
k = discount rate

Source: Leibowitz, Sorensen, Arnott, and Hanson, *A Total Differential Approach to Equity Duration* (New York: Salomon Brothers Inc, 1987).

expression for DDM duration emerges. The duration is a number whose magnitude and evaluation should be important.

What does this formula mean for the stock market? If there is an increase in interest rates, and the discount rate (k) increases by the same amount, and nothing else happens—for instance, no growth interaction and no risk premium changes—the valuation response will be significant. Let us look at a numerical example. Currently, I use an average discount rate of 13 percent—the rate varies from 11 to 20 percent, depending on how risky the stock is (Sorensen and Kreichman, 1987). That is an average rate for all stocks made up of the long-term bond rate plus a risk premium. I assume an average growth rate of 8.5 to 9 percent; let us use 9 percent. So incorporating those numbers into the formula, the stock market should have a 25 percent decline in value for every 100 basis point rise in rates $(1/(.13-.09) = 1/.04)$. That certainly did not happen between January and July of 1987. This rather partial, simplistic way of looking at duration for stocks is important, however; it is well-founded, but it may not be the whole answer.

Is DDM stock duration relevant? Theoretically, it is relevant for dividend-paying stocks. The formula for DDM duration for dividend-paying stocks is presented in Figure 7. The

market dividend yield is about 3 percent: therefore the market duration is estimated to be 33 years, using this formula. This may be relevant for companies that have constant growth and no change in the risk premium, as the model assumes. The model lacks the interactive dynamic for total interest-rate sensitivity, however.

A different way of examining stock duration is to consider the total impact of interest-rate change—not just the partial relationship—based

FIGURE 7. DDM Duration for Dividend-Paying Stocks

$$k-g = D/P$$

$$D_{DDM} = \frac{1}{D/P}$$

$$= \frac{1}{YIELD}$$

where:

k = discount rate
g = growth rate
D/P = dividend yield

Source: Leibowitz, Sorensen, Arnott, and Hanson, *A Total Differential Approach to Equity Duration* (New York: Salomon Brothers Inc, 1987).

on a valuation formula that includes dynamics, a model that specifies how the earnings growth and the equity market risk premium changes (Leibowitz, Sorensen, Arnott, and Hanson, 1987). Two of the issues which must be resolved are: Why are there three different measures of duration? And, are they consistent? Figure 8 presents a set of simplifying assumptions. The first assumption, a CAPM type of specification, is that the rate of return on equities should be related to a nominal interest rate plus a risk premium. The second assumption, which is essentially the Fisher effect, is that the nominal rate of interest—which in turn is a part of the discount rate for equities—is a function of the inflationary expectations plus a real rate of interest. Third, the corporate growth rate is assumed to be equal to some constant long-term growth rate plus two components that change: One is a flow-through component, and the other is a real-interest-rate component.

FIGURE 8. Simplifying Assumptions

$$i)\; k = i + h\; (l, r....)$$
$$ii)\; i = r + l$$
$$iii)\; g = g_o + r + \lambda l$$

where:

i	=	the nominal interest rate
h	=	equity market risk premium
r	=	a real component to nominal rates
l	=	inflation component of nominal rates
g_o	=	constant growth parameter
γ	=	growth rate sensitivity to real interest rates
λ	=	inflation flowthrough parameter

Source: Leibowitz, Sorensen, Arnott, and Hanson, *A Total Differential Approach to Equity Duration* (New York: Salomon Brothers Inc, 1987).

Figure 9 illustrates an analytical solution to the stock duration calculation. It may look a little frightening—in fact, it is a simplified version. The total differential of price with respect to the stock's valuation is the last equation (Leibowitz, Sorensen, Arnott, and Hanson, 1987). The previous DDM duration models implied partial—not total—derivatives. The partial related only to changes in the discount rate. The new model considers the total differential in price related to both growth and the risk premium, and the interactions between those changes and interest rates. The interest-rate sensitivity is the total differential of the price of a stock with respect to interest-rate change, which could be the formula for DDM duration. The figure shows a negative sign because there is an inverse relationship between duration (which is a positive number) and a change in price or a change in interest rates (which is a negative number).

When would the formula in Figure 9 be the DDM duration? Valuation duration measures may be very appropriate if nominal interest rates and real interest rates do not influence earnings growth, and if the risk premium is constant. The first component says one of two

FIGURE 9. Analytical Solution

Derivation of the formula:

$$P = \frac{D_o}{k - g}$$

$$\ln P = \ln D_o - \ln\; (k - g)$$

$$\frac{dp}{P} = d\ln P = \frac{\partial \ln P}{\partial k} dk + \frac{\partial \ln P}{\partial g} dg = -\frac{1}{k - g}(dk - dg) = -D_{ddm}(dk - dg)$$

From Figure 8,

$$dk = dr + dl + \frac{\partial h}{\partial l} dl + \frac{\partial h}{\partial r} dr$$

$$dg = \gamma\, dr + \lambda\, dl$$

Thus,

$$\frac{dP}{P} = -D_{DDM}\left(1 - \gamma + \frac{\partial h}{\partial r}\right) dr - D_{DDM}\left(1 - \lambda + \frac{\partial h}{\gamma l}\right) dl$$

or the following two components:

$$-D_{DDM}\left(1 - \gamma + \frac{\partial h}{\partial r}\right) = \text{sensitivity to changes in the real rate of interest.}$$

$$-D_{DDM}\left(1 - \lambda + \frac{\partial h}{\partial l}\right) = \text{sensitivity to changes in interest rates resulting from changes in inflation expectations.}$$

Source: Leibowitz, Sorensen, Arnott, and Hanson, *A Total Differential Approach to Equity Duration* (New York: Salomon Brothers Inc, 1987).

things: either the coefficients and interactions do not count, or, alternatively, that there is no change in the real rate. We are not experiencing a real rate change. Therefore, the interest-rate sensitivity component is DDM duration; it is 20 years. The second term relates to nominal sensitivities. It says that if we have inflation acceleration or change in inflation (which causes the nominal interest rate to change), and the inflation flow-through is zero (and that the risk premium does not change), then the term in the brackets is also zero; and the duration is 20 years.

For the dividend discount model, duration is meaningful only if we combine the DDM measure in this type of formulation with the interactive effects. Using statistical procedures to measure the relevant sensitivities, we can derive a more meaningful number for the total sensitivity of stock price change to interest-rate change.

SOME MARKETS HAVE LARGER DURATIONS

Let us look at some examples to clarify the meaning of this approach. Figure 10 compares the DDM duration model without interaction terms with one that has interaction terms. The top calculation is the one referred to earlier in this presentation. The second calculation considers the effect of inflation flow-through. Based on our calculations, the average effect of inflation on corporate earnings is between 0.7 and 0.9; in some industries it is more, in some it is less. In some it is more reliable; in some it is less reliable—that is, the R-squares are not always high. On average, inflation flow-through might be 0.8. If it were 0.8, then the interactive effect will put downward pressure on the DDM duration; the analytical solution is 5 rather than 25. For a 100 basis point move in interest rates, there would be a 5 percent decline in stock prices because of this interaction effect. (The influence of interest-rate change on present value is largely offset by an opposite impact of inflation on earnings growth.)

Another interactive effect is the relationship between the change in corporate growth and the change in the real rate of interest. In a tight money environment, there would be an escalation in the real cost of credit—or more strictly, shortage of credit. There may not be any benefits in terms of profitability, so shortage of credit

---

FIGURE 10. Example of Analytical Solution

A. Inflation Flowthrough

  Assume:
  $$g = .10$$
  $$k = .14$$
  $$\lambda = .8$$
  $$dl = 100 \text{ basis points}$$
  $$dr = 0$$

  Then,

  $$D_{DDM} = \frac{1}{k-g} = \frac{1}{.04} = 25$$

  with inflation flowthrough,

  $$\frac{\Delta P}{P} = -D_{DDM}(1-\lambda)\Delta l$$

  $$= -25(1-0.8)(1\%)$$

  $$= -5\%$$

B. Change in Real Rates

  Assume:
  $$\gamma = -.2$$
  $$dr = 100 \text{ basis points}$$
  $$dl = 0$$

  $$\frac{\Delta P}{P} = -D_{DDM}(1-\gamma)\Delta r$$

  $$= +25(1+0.2)(1\%)$$

  $$= -30\%$$

Source: Leibowitz, Sorensen, Arnott, and Hanson, *A Total Differential Approach to Equity Duration* (New York: Salomon Brothers Inc, 1987).

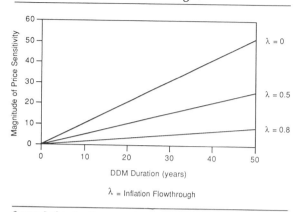

FIGURE 11. Price Sensitivity vs. DDM Duration for Different Flowthroughs

λ = Inflation Flowthrough

Source: Leibowitz, Sorensen, Arnott, and Hanson, *A Total Differential Approach to Equity Duration* (New York: Salomon Brothers Inc, 1987).

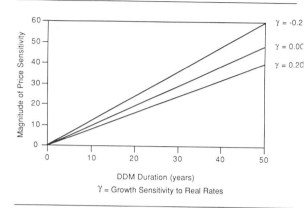

FIGURE 12. Price Sensitivity vs. DDM Duration for Different Real Rate Sensitivities

γ = Growth Sensitivity to Real Rates

Source: Leibowitz, Sorensen, Arnott, and Hanson, *A Total Differential Approach to Equity Duration* (New York: Salomon Brothers Inc, 1987).

really cuts into the profit margins. In this case, an increase in real rates is associated with a dramatic response in stock prices, as illustrated in Figure 10.

Figures 11 and 12 illustrate the price sensitivity versus the DDM duration using flow-through and real interest-rate sensitivity. Figure 11 shows that in all likelihood, stock-price sensitivity to inflation is less than DDM duration. For a flow-through of 0.8, the highest durations would be five to eight years, at most.

Figure 12 presents a very different picture. A change in real interest rates probably has an impact on growth ranging from −0.20 to +0.20, depending upon what caused the change in rates. If monetary policy caused the rise in rates, then the sensitivity of growth is likely to be negative. If economic stimulation (credit demand) caused the rise in rates, then the sensitivity of growth may be positive. In either case, Figure 12 illustrates that changes in real interest rates are synonymous with a large duration impact for stocks.

It is thus possible to consider periods when the financial markets might be characterized as a high duration environment for stock as opposed to a "low duration environment. The stock market will behave like a long duration asset if: (1) the change in rates is real as opposed to nominal; (2) companies have low levels of inflation flow-through; or (3) the equity market risk premium is moving in the same direction as interest rates. We may now refer back to Figures 3, 4, and 5 and use the equations to confirm our

visual analysis. For example, the period 1982-87 was a high duration period because, although interest rates fell, earnings growth was well intact for most companies. As another example, the credit crisis environments of 1969 and 1974 were periods of high real interest rates, creating large downward pressure on stock valuations.

SOME STOCKS HAVE LARGER DURATIONS

Just as some market environments have high duration potential, certain stocks (or industry groups) have longer durations than others. Drawing from the price change equations, stocks with long durations would have (1) high growth potential; (2) stable earnings patterns over time; and (3) less earnings sensitivity to either changes in real interest rates or inflation.

Food stocks are an example of long duration stocks, as illustrated in Figures 13, 14, and 15. In Figure 13, the price of food stocks rose while interest rates fell. Earnings are relatively constant: over the long term, they have not borne much of a relationship to interest rates. This indicates that in the case of food stocks, the P/E pattern is a function of interest-rate change; and as such these stocks participated in the duration move of 1982-87.

The low duration example is taken from the forest products industry. Figures 16, 17, and 18 illustrate the relationship between interest rates and price, and earnings and P/E, respectively. Looking at Figure 16, prices increase more or

FIGURE 13. Food Stocks: Price

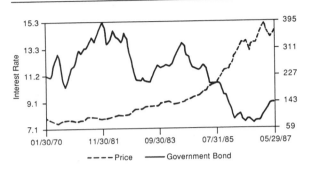

Source: Eric H. Sorensen

FIGURE 16. Forest Products: Price

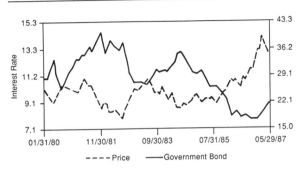

Source: Eric H. Sorensen

FIGURE 14. Food Stocks: EPS

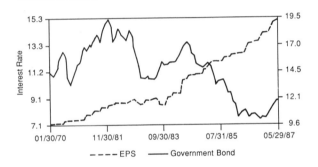

Source: Eric H. Sorensen

FIGURE 17. Forest Products: EPS

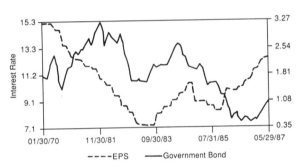

Source: Eric H. Sorensen

FIGURE 15. Food Stocks: P/E

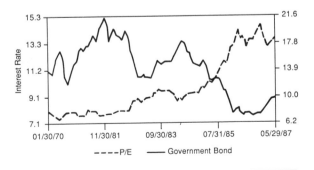

Source: Eric H. Sorensen

FIGURE 18. Forest Products: P/E

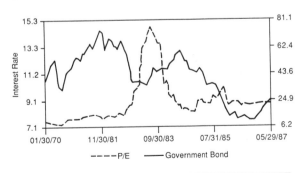

Source: Eric H. Sorensen

less, but not necessarily when rates change. Forest product earnings are highly cyclical. They are also highly leveraged. Earnings appear to fall with interest rates. This is not an example of a group which would have long duration characteristics. It is harder to model. The interaction effects are more important. In sum, the P/E is fairly flat, and the group might be better thought of as an earnings play. At the same time, foods might be thought of as an interest-rate play.

DURATION FACTOR PERFORMANCE

To examine the performance of duration measures in a multifactor context, we analyzed some historical return data. The performance analysis was a two-stage process. First, we ran a cross-sectional regression for a large number of stocks in which monthly return was the dependent variable, and several factors (or security attributes) made up the independent variables. A measure of duration constituted one of the independent variables.

Figure 19 presents a graph of the duration contribution to returns on a monthly basis beginning in December 1976. The lower line in Figure 19 is a cumulative measure of the monthly regression coefficients attributable to the duration measure. If the line is rising, high duration stocks are outperforming low duration stocks.

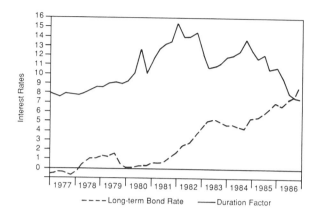

FIGURE 19. Effective Strategy Performance: Duration Factor Index

Source: Eric H. Sorensen

Figure 19 also presents a history of the long-term bond rate. It is apparent that long duration stocks had relatively high returns during the 1981-86 period. This coincided with the major fall in interest rates over the same period.

In conclusion, I believe that duration for stocks will continue to be of interest to investors and portfolio strategists. The increasing trend toward quantitative strategies, and the need to use common factors which transcend multiple asset classes, make duration an important area of future research.

Question and Answer Session

QUESTION: Because most book value data is greatly influenced by accounting techniques and the maturity of the company (it is not stated nominally), how can one effectively use it in a T-model?

ESTEP: In a certain sense, it does not make any difference. As preposterous as this sounds, the relationship of the T-model to return is really independent of whether the accounting numbers are right or not. It is just an identity. It is true even if the numbers are totally bizarre, provided that they are stated in the same way at the end of the holding period as they were at the beginning of the holding period. That answer, however, is not very satisfactory. To compensate, analysts must do two things in real life: first, make an effort to get comparable numbers across companies; and second, because it is impossible to get comparable numbers across industries, be very careful about comparing expected returns across industries. It is much safer to make expected return comparisons within an industry.

QUESTION: Why don't more firms use performance fees, especially if they could add the value presupposed?

FOGLER: We use performance fees. We write them against the S&P 500. Initially, coming out of academics, I thought that performance fees would make one sharper and a harder worker. There is also merit to the argument that performance fees won't have much impact; and I'm not sure that they have any effect on our performance. But they do tell potential clients that we believe in what we say.

Anyway, all contracts are performance contracts; only the horizon differs. After three years, if we do not perform well, we are going to be fired. And if we do produce well—e.g. if we produced a risk-adjusted 800 basis points over the S&P 500 and if we could *guarantee* to produce 800 basis points in the future—clients are going to pay more than our current fees.

QUESTION: How do you estimate the change in the price/book ratio? And if you can estimate that, why do you need a T-model or any other model?

ESTEP: If you could estimate price in the short term you would not need a model. The returns on the S&P 500 can be decomposed—on both the individual stock and the portfolio—into growth, cashflow, and valuation change. Over a long period of time, the mean return from growth on the S&P 500 is 8 or 9 percent, and the mean return from cashflow yield is around 3.5 percent. They both have modest standard deviations. The mean return from valuation change approaches zero, as it ought to. The price/book ratio of the S&P 500 has grown dramatically in the past five years, but it probably cannot grow without limit. So over a long time, it has a large standard deviation and a small mean, and does not contribute much to return. On the other hand, growth has a large mean and a modest standard deviation and cashflow yield has a smaller mean and a smaller deviation. Based on these three terms, the T-model is always true. It is true even over a day. In one day, a firm grows very little and has a small cashflow yield. So the return in a day is all valuation change. The return in a year is still heavily influenced by valuation change. But as time goes on, the importance of valuation change is less and less, and it reverts to a mean of zero, so that this whole process is only good for one of two kinds of investors: a long-term investor who is willing to ride out swings in valuation change and invest for the sum of the first few terms, and an investor who can make some conjectural estimate of valuation change—and the better it is, the more short-term oriented the results can be.

QUESTION: Has the standard deviation of the market portfolio return distribution increased over time, or has it become more skewed?

FOGLER: This is a totally subjective answer, but I do not think anything changes much over long periods of say 50 years. Most changes are really noise, although shorter subperiods of 5 or 10 years may be quite different in their characteristics. It is more important to determine whether there are fundamental changes in earnings. Statisticians know that the estimation error on distribution parameters is huge.

QUESTION: What is the S&P 500 duration?

SORENSEN: It is approximately 10—ranging between 8 and 11; depending on how it is measured.

QUESTION: Are you assuming that stocks are only sensitive to interest rates, while other influences do not matter? Bond duration is estimated to capture 80 to 90 percent of the total return for bonds. What is the comparable number for equities?

SORENSEN: No. Interest rates are not the only influence. The major force out there is corporate uncertainty. Bonds have an asymmetrical distribution. With rising rates, mostly only bad things can happen, and very little that is good. You do not get the top end of the corporate profitability distribution. But with a stock, you get that. But that is nonsystematic. And at the other extreme one would never say that stocks are 80 to 90 percent driven by interest rate changes. There are environments, however, where there is a very high correlation between interest rate movements and stock price movements. But there is also a great variance.

I could divide the S&P 500 into three groups based on my ability to calculate duration. There is a group of stocks about which I am comfortable discussing duration. This group is basically predictable, and the duration may be high. In the second group, the duration may not be very high but it is sort of predictable. Finally, there is a group, which is primarily earnings-driven, where it is hard to model duration because it is hard to predict earnings. Thus, my answer really depends on the group and the time frame.

Relative Valuation of International Equity Markets: The Japanese Example

Paul H. Aron

I first became involved with Japanese securities in 1969, when I made what at that time was the largest investment for an open-ended American mutual fund in Japanese securities—well over $100 million. I was told that I had made a dreadful mistake: "The Tokyo Dow is now at its high point—1851. It has topped out. The market is too pricy. It is in for a huge correction." The last time I looked, the Nikkei index (formerly the Tokyo Dow) exceeded 20,000.

We have consistently received reports that the Japanese market is overpriced. From April 3, 1981 until August 31, 1987, the S&P 500 has grown 149.1 percent; the Nikkei Dow Jones Average has grown 245.5 percent; and the Tokyo Stock Exchange Index 290.3 percent. When those figures are converted into U.S. dollars, however, the Nikkei has grown 421.8 percent, and the Tokyo Stock Exchange has grown 488.7 percent. Table 1 shows the history.

It is important that Americans understand what is happening in Japan. The difference in accounting principles is one area that should be studied. My views on the investment potential of Japanese companies differ from those of many investment managers for two reasons. First, contrary to popular opinion and despite the growing Americanization of Japanese accounting standards, the reported Japanese earnings per share are still significantly understated, although the understatement is far less substantial than it was in the 1960s. When Japanese earnings per share are recalculated to conform with U.S. accounting standards, they are 76.1 percent higher than reported earnings per share. In the September 1987 issue, *Morgan Stanley Capital International Perspective* (MSCIP) reported a Japanese price/earnings (P/E) ratio of 62.9, compared to the American P/E of 20.3. Using American accounting standards, however, the Japanese P/E ratio was only 33.9 times,

only 53.9 percent of the P/E ratio reported by Morgan Stanley.[1]

Second, when a common accounting standard is used, Japanese corporations earn less profit per unit of market value than their American counterparts. When Japanese earnings are adjusted to conform to U.S. generally accepted accounting principles (GAAP) and are capitalized on the same basis as U.S. earnings, the P/E ratios are very similar. As of August 31, 1987, the adjusted average Japanese P/E ratio was 17.2; the corresponding U.S. P/E ratio was 20.3.

I believe that in the future, American security analysts will cover not just U.S. industries and their companies, but all significant companies regardless of their geographic location, and place them on a single accounting and capitalization foundation. The portfolio manager will invest in the best companies in the most promising industries, taking full account of the relevant economic differences in each country.

I would like to discuss several conclusions that I have reached about international equity investing. I am fully aware that these conclusions are tentative and require much further analysis and observation. I am by no means dogmatic; I will try to show alternative explanations.

I would like to begin by posing a question that is central to the whole issue of international investing, using Japan as an example: Is the price/earnings ratio of the Japanese stock market, whatever its level, justified by the outlook for Japan's future? Is Japan really a fragile blossom, as one professor who later became the head of the U.S. National Security Council predicted in the early 1970s, or will it continue to be an iron chrysanthemum, overcoming new ob-

[1] The analysis in this presentation is based on Paul Aron Report #31, *Japanese Price Earnings Multiples: Updated as of August 31, 1987*. New York: Daiwa Securities America Inc., 1987. For additional information, see Paul Aron Report Nos. 24 (1981), 27 (1984), 29 (1986), and 30 (1987).

TABLE 1. Growth of American and Japanese Equity Markets

		8/31/87	*4/30/81*	*8/31/84*	*2/28/86*	*3/31/87*	*8/31/87*	*4/30/81-8/31/87* *% increase*
U.S.	Dow Jones		997.75	1,224.38	1,709.06	2,304.69	2,662.95	166.9%
	S&P 500		132.81	166.68	226.92	291.70	330.85	149.1%
Japan	Nikkei Average (Yen)		7,534.41	10,584.20	13,640.83	21,566.66	26,029.22	245.5%
	Tokyo Stock Exchange Index (Yen)		551.91	816.69	1,090.70	1,871.19	2,154.26	290.3%
	Yen/Dollar Exchange Rate		215.00	241.70	180.45	145.65	142.35	
	Nikkei Average (US$)		35.04	43.79	75.59	148.07	182.85	421.8%
	Tokyo Stock Exchange Index (US$)		2.57	3.38	6.04	12.85	15.13	488.7%

Source: Daiwa Securities America Inc.

stacles as it did in the 1970s during the twin Arab oil shocks.[2] That is the basic thesis of this presentation.

Throughout this presentation I have used the Morgan Stanley Capital International Indexes as the basis for illustrating American investment managers' misconceptions about Japanese securities. Their Japan index consists of 238 stocks. Although I have noted certain inaccuracies in the calculation of this index in the past, I believe that the figures are accurate now. One fact, however, should be noted. Morgan Stanley's index does not seem to adjust for conversion of outstanding convertible debentures and warrants, although they currently adjust for rights offerings.

The MSCIP index illustrates a few problems that most Americans have in analyzing Japanese financial information. A number of adjustments must be made to the index so that it is comparable with American indexes. I will use the Morgan Stanley index to illustrate the type of adjustments that must be made.

The first adjustment involves accounting for non-life insurance companies and differences in consolidation. Japanese non-life insurance companies, or what we call property and casualty companies in the United States, use statuatory accounting which is cash accounting. This means that if a policy is signed the day before the balance sheet closes, all the expenses are charged to that year; then, over time, as the cash comes in, income is generated. Morgan Stanley uses the Japanese method of statuatory earnings: Daiwa converts these companies to U.S.

GAAP. The difference between statutory and GAAP earnings for the four companies in the index averaged 178.48 percent, e.g., the Japanese are understating earnings by that amount. This results in an adjustment factor of 3 percent to the index.

The MSCIP index includes 33 companies whose financial results have not been fully consolidated. Thus, the index must be adjusted for the consolidated earnings. The results of a study of the 724 companies in the Tokyo Stock Exchange indicate that the earnings understatement is 11.08 percent. That is the figure I am using to adjust the Morgan Stanley Index for the difference between consolidated and parent earnings.

These modifications to make the MSCIP Index conform to U.S. GAAP involve an adjustment of 4.54 percent. This results in the earnings per share (EPS) increasing from $1.59 to $1.66 and the price/earnings ratio decreasing from 62.9 to 60.2, as illustrated in Table 2.

Although Japanese accounting has been steadily Americanized over the past decade, a number of differences still remain. These differences must be incorporated into any analysis of EPS. One important difference between the two countries is tax law. Japan is characterized by tax conformity; tax deductions are permitted only if they have been recognized in reports to the stockholders either before or concurrently with tax recognition. In contrast, American companies may issue two different reports: one to the stockholder and one to the tax authorities, enabling them to maximize reported earnings per share to the stockholders and minimize taxable income on their tax returns. Japanese

---

[2] Brzezinski, Zbigniew. *The Fragile Blossom—Crisis and Change in Japan*, Harper & Row, 1972.

TABLE 2. Adjustment For Life Insurance and Parent Consolidation

Adjustments:	A Number of Companies	B % of Universe A/238	C Margin of Adjustments	D Adjustment [B × C]
1. GAAP Adjustment for Non-Life Insurance Companies	4	1.68%	178.48%	3.00%
2. Consolidation adjustment for parent only	33	13.87%	11.08%	1.54%
Total	37			4.54%

Price/Earnings Ratio Adjustment:	U.S.	Japan
A. Assumed Stock Price	$100.00	$100.00
B. Price Earnings Ratio	20.30 Times	62.9 times
C. Earnings Per Share (EPS)	$ 4.93	$ 1.59
D. Adjustment for Differences with MSCIP (4.54% × 1.59)		0.07
E. EPS Adjusted for Differences with MSCIP		1.66
F. PER Adjusted for Differences with MSCIP ($100/E)		60.2 times

Source: Daiwa Securities America Inc.

companies may only file one report. Both reports use the same figures with one exception: the tax authority has a limit on the amount of entertainment expense that may be deducted. Therefore, the tax authority financial statements only show the amount of the entertainment deduction allowed; in the stockholder statements, the full entertainment expense is deducted. For some companies, the earnings per share may be lower in the report to the stockholders than in the report to the tax authorities.

Japanese tax law also provides for a wide variety of general and special purpose reserves, which from an American point of view are essentially untaxed earnings. The general purpose reserves apply to nearly all Japanese companies, and are usually not changed from year to year. The two most important of these are the reserve for bad debt and the reserve for retirement payments. In addition to writing off their bad debt every year, Japanese companies are permitted to establish a reserve for bad debt which far exceeds their actual experience.

The retirement process is different in Japan. In a Japanese firm, the normal retirement age is between 55 and 60, except for senior executives. Also, in a Japanese company, retired employees usually do not stop working; they may continue to work for the firm or one of its subsidiaries. They are no longer entitled to guaranteed employment, however, and may be laid off if business becomes slow. Of course, some people choose to work for themselves when they get their retirement money. The retirement payment is actually a deferred wage payable on the employee's departure from the firm, usually in the form of one or two month's wages for each year of service. Retirees may receive as much as 80 months pay in one shot, tax free. Japanese companies expense the actual annual retirement payments. In addition, the company may create a reserve equal to 40 percent of its liability, assuming that all employees retired at balance sheet date, which is also deducted from pretax income. This is only a bookkeeping entry; the money is not separately funded in a retirement pay account. Pension funds are beginning to develop in Japan, but the bulk of Japanese retirement is still based on this reserve.

There are also general reserves for goods returned; there are reserves for special repairs; there are often large reserves for product guarantees—although there appears to be little need for a product guarantee reserve because of the quality of Japanese products.

The special purpose reserves are generally designated annually by the government, which identifies the branches of the economy that it wishes to promote. These special reserves may change from year to year. There are reserves for overseas market development, overseas investment loss, and computer repurchase loss. The hydroelectric plants have two reserves: one for dry weather, and one of almost equal size for excessive moisture. There are also reserves for computer programs.

TABLE 3. Adjustment For Additions To Reserves

A. Addition to Long-term Reserve	338 Yen (in millions)
B. Addition to Special Reserve	(9)
C. Total Addition to Reserves (A+B)	329
D. Deferred Taxes at (52.92% × C)	174
E. Net Addition to Reserves After Taxes (C−D)	155
F. Reported Net Income	2,662
G. Net Parent Reserves as a % of Reported Net Income (E/F)	5.82%
H. EPS as Corrected for MSCIP Differences	$1.66
I. Adjustment for Reserves (5.82% × $1.66)	0.10
J. EPS Adjusted for MSCIP Differences and Reserves	1.76
K. PER Adjusted for MSCIP Differences and Reserves ($100/J)	56.8 times

Source: Analysts' Guide, Daiwa Securities Co., Tokyo, 1987.

A special depreciation reserve allows an additional deduction for special machinery—for example an extra 12.5 percent results in a 52.5 percent depreciation in the first year versus 40 percent for double declining method, and 20 percent for the straight line method (which is rarely used in Japan). This extra depreciation may be taken over the course of five years, with pay-back beginning in the sixth year—except if in the sixth year, the company purchases a new machine which is priced higher than the first, in which case the special reserve is not really paid back. There is even a special reserve now that provides an allowance for buying American equipment. This special additional depreciation allowance ranges from 8 percent to 36 percent.

The special reserve seems to be gradually losing its importance. To measure the impact of these reserves, however, we use a book called the *Analyst's Guide*, issued by Daiwa Securities Research Institute. The book has been issued since 1970; it provides information on five fiscal years, the last one ending on March 31, 1987. It covers 1,405 companies on a parent company basis. The book excludes financial companies. For the five-year period from March 1983 to March 1987, the net addition to reserves increased over 20.5 percent.

Table 3 shows the addition to long-term and special reserves for the fiscal year ending March 31, 1987. The analysis is on an aftertax basis, assuming a tax rate of 52.92 percent. In this way, the actual net addition to aftertax earnings can be determined. The reserve adjustment causes net income to be modified by $.10 per share. Remember, the base was $1.66. Now the net income is $1.76, and the price/earnings ratio is 56.8 times.

The next adjustment is for differences in consolidation, illustrated in Table 4. Consolidation was once a big factor; that is no longer true. Nevertheless, despite the Ministry of Finance rulings that require consolidation reporting, corporations still issue parent company reports, and these parent company reports are usually released earlier than consolidated reports. They will probably be issued simultaneously within the next year or two. The Ministry of Finance regulations on consolidation have an escape clause, however: Subsidiaries that constitute less than 10 percent of net consolidated income, or less than 10 percent of consolidated sales, or

TABLE 4. Adjustment for Consolidation

A. EPS adjusted for MSCIP differences and reserves			$ 1.76
B. Adjustment of EPS for non-consolidated EPS (5% × 1.76)			0.09
C. EPS adjusted for MSCIP differences, reserves, and non-consolidated EPS			1.85
D. Adjustment of EPS for reserves of consolidated and non-consolidated companies (0.93% × 1.85)			
− For consolidated co. 11.08% × 5.82%	0.64%		
− For non-consolidated co. 5% × 5.82%	0.29%		
Total	0.93%		
E. EPS adjusted for MSCIP differences, reserves, and consolidation			1.87
F. PER adjusted for differences, reserves, and consolidation ($100/E)			53.5 times

Source: Daiwa Securities America Inc.

TABLE 5. Adjustment for Method of Calculating EPS	
A. EPS as previously adjusted for MSCIP differences and accounting differences	$ 1.87
B. Adjustment for changing from shares at year-end to annual average (.8% × 1.87)	0.02
C. EPS adjusted for MSCIP differences, accounting difference in reserves, consolidation, and method of calculating EPS ($100/C)	1.89
D. PER adjusted for MSCIP differences, accounting difference in reserves, consolidation, and the method of calculating EPS ($100/C)	52.9 Times

Source: Daiwa Securities America Inc.

less than 10 percent of consolidated assets, may be ignored in the consolidated statement. The Japanese have been very adept at calculating the 10 percent value: subsidiaries that are not reported often represent 9.999 percent of consolidated figures. To be conservative, I use 5 percent to adjust earnings for nonconsolidated companies instead of 10 percent. But the reserves of both the consolidated and the nonconsolidated subsidiaries must be included, adding another $.02 per share. Thus, after adjusting for consolidation differences, the P/E ratio has dropped to 53.5 times.

An adjustment must be made for differences in calculating earnings per share. The Japanese calculate earnings per share on the basis of the number of shares outstanding at the time that the financial report is issued. This contrasts with the American method of averaging shares outstanding over the fiscal year. I calculated that the total number of shares increased by 1.6 percent over the year because of new issues. Assuming an equal monthly increase, the adjustment is 0.8 percent. This brings earnings per share to $1.89, and the price/earnings ratio to 52.9, as shown in Table 5.

Finally, the earnings figures must be adjusted for differences in reported depreciation. American companies may use accelerated depreciation for tax reports, and straight line depreciation for financial reports. Most Japanese firms, because they file only one report, choose to use accelerated depreciation rather than straight line depreciation, thereby reducing taxes. This results in lower stated earnings on the financial statements compared to U.S. statements.

To calculate the understatement for depreciation, we use a formula suggested by Mr. Yamana, CFA, former chairman of Daiwa Securities America. The Japanese managers seek to expense as much of their costs as possible, and therefore report a rate of depreciation which is excessive by American standards. Mr. Yamana's formula assumes a rate of cash flow to depreci-

TABLE 6. Adjustment for Excess Depreciation	U.S.	Japan
A. Assumed Stock Price	$100.0	$100.0
B. Price/Earnings Ratio	20.3 times	62.9 times
C. Earnings Per Share	$ 4.93	$ 1.59
D. Price/Cash Flow (P/CF)	9.5 times	15.7 times
E. Cash Flow Per Share	$ 10.53	$ 6.37
F. Depreciation Per Share (E–C)	5.60	4.78
G. Excess Depreciation Per Share (see formula)	0.00	1.94
H. Deferred Tax Per Share (.53 × G)	0.00	1.03
I. Latent Earnings Per Share (G–H)	0.00	0.91
J. True Cash Flow Per Share (E–H)	10.53	5.34
K. True Depreciation Per Share (F–G)	5.60	2.84
L. Adjustment for excess depreciation of consolidated (11.08%) and nonconsolidated companies (5.00%): 16.08 × .91 = .15	0.00	0.15
M. EPS adjusted for MSCIP differences and differences in accounting and depreciation	4.93	$ 2.95
N. PER adjusted for MSCIP differences and differences in accounting and depreciation	20.3 times	33.9 times

Source: Daiwa Securities America Inc.

TABLE 7. Adjustment for Differences in Capitalization Rate

	U.S.	Japan
A. Riskless rate = yield of 10-year government bonds	8.9%	4.56%
B. Earnings yield-PER of riskless rate (1/A1 for US, 1/A2 for Japan)	11.15 Times	21.95 Times
C. Japanese PER/U.S. PER of riskless rate (21.95/11.15)	—	1.97
D. EPS fully adjusted for MSCIP differences and accounting differences	$ 4.93	$ 3.32
E. PER fully adjusted for MSCIP differences and accounting differences	20.3 Times	33.9 Times
F. PER fully adjusted for MSCIP differences and accounting differences and capitalization differences (35.7/1.97)	20.3	17.2

TABLE 8. Summary as of August 31, 1987

Revised	U.S.	Amount of Adjustment	Japan
A. Stock Price	$ 100.00		$ 100.00
B. PER	20.30 Times		62.90 Times
C. EPS	$ 4.93		$ 1.59
D. Adjustment for differences with MSCIP ...... (4.54% × 1.59)		0.07	1.66

	A Number of Companies	B % of Universe A/238	C Margin of Adjustments	D Adjustment [B × C]
1. Statutory rather than GAAP EPS [See accompanying Table 2]	4	1.68%	178.49%	3.00%
2. Consolidation adjustment for parent only reports.	33	13.87%	11.08%	1.54%
	37			4.54%

			Amount of Adjustment	Japan
E. Adjustment for Reserves	5.82% ×	1.66	0.10	1.76
F. Adjustment for non-consolidated EPS	5.00% ×	1.76	0.09	1.85
G. Adj. for reserves of consolidated co.	5.82% × 11.08%	0.64%		
H. Adj. for reserves of non-consol. co.	5.82% × 5.00%	0.29%		
	0.93% ×	1.85	0.02	1.87
I. Adjustment for shares at year end not averaged	0.81% ×	1.87	0.02	1.89
J. Adjustment for understated depreciation			1.06	2.95
K. Total of All Adjustments			1.36	
L. PER—adjusted for accounting differences		20.3 Times		33.9 Times
M. PER adjustment for differences in accounting and capitalization rate	33.9 / 1.97	20.3		17.2

Source: Daiwa Securities America Inc.

ation in Japan to be the same as in the United States (see Exhibit 1). Cash flow is assumed to be 1.8 times depreciation in the United States and 1.33 times in Japan. To place Japan on the same standard of depreciation would require that cash flow equal 1.88 times depreciation.

The Japanese financial statements have $1.94 of hidden earnings which they have labeled improperly by American standards. The aftertax latent earnings are $.91. Thus, if we apply the same standards of depreciation to United States and Japanese companies, the Japanese earnings per share would include $.91 of latent earnings net after taxes, reported as depreciation. In addition, we must take into account the understated depreciation of the consolidated and non-consolidated companies. Using 11.08 percent for the consolidated and 5 percent for the non-consolidated companies, we derive .15 (16.08 x .91). Table 6 shows the earnings of the Japanese companies earned $2.95 per share, reducing the PER to 33.9 times. No adjustment has been made for write-off of intangibles and goodwill, or for the absence of capitalized expense. This reflects both our conservatism and the difficulty of quantification. Japanese corporations still expense intangible assets rapidly, and intangible assets represent less than 0.01 percent of the total fixed assets of the companies. At this point, Japanese and American earnings are on the same accounting basis.

The final step is to adjust for differences in the capitalization rate (see Table 7). In the U.S., the yield on a 10-year bond on the secondary market was 8.97 percent. Assuming that this is the riskless rate of return, we paid 11 times for riskless earnings in the United States. In Japan, the 10-year government bond rate on the secondary market was 4.56 percent in August, and so the Japanese were paying almost 22 times for riskless investment. It is my belief that if a riskless investment in Japan sells at twice the rate of a risky investment, then we must calculate the equity investment on that same basis. I have taken the 33.9 times earnings, divided by 1.97, which is the difference in the riskless rate, resulting in a P/E ratio of 17.2. When all adjustments are made, the P/E ratio of 17.2 in Japan is not terribly different from the 20.3 ratio in the United States (as summarized in Table 8). Thus the Japanese market, with its somewhat lower P/E ratio, seems less vulnerable that the United States market.

Exhibit 1

CALCULATION OF DEPRECIATION

Cash Flow and Depreciation Per Share — U.S.

Cash Flow (E) = 10.53
Depreciation (F) = 5.60

E/F = 10.53/5.60 = 1.88

E = 1.88 × F

Cash Flow and Depreciation Per Share — Japan

Reported Cash Flow (E) = 6.37
Reported Depreciation (F) = 4.78

E/F = 6.37 × 4.78 = 1.33

E = 1.33 × F

Assuming that Japanese managers use their discretion to allocate depreciation in the same manner as the U.S. Then,

| True Cash Flow (J) = 1.88 × True Depreciation (K) | J = 1.88 × K |

But the excess depreciation converted into earnings would be subject to corporate income tax (53%). Therefore,

| True Depreciation (K) = Reported Depreciation (F) – Excess Depreciation (G) | K = F − G |

| Deferred Tax on Excess Depreciation (H) = .53 × Excess Depreciation (G) | H = .53 × G |

| True Cash Flow (J) = Reported Cash Flow (E) – Deferred Tax on Excess Depreciation (H) | J = E − H |

| Reported Cash Flow (E) = True Cash Flow (J) + Deferred Tax on Excess Depreciation (H) | E = J + H |

| Latent earnings (I) = Excess Depreciation (G) – Deferred Tax on Excess Depreciation (H) | I = G − H |

Using the above formulas, we can solve for G (excess depreciation).

1.   E = J + H
2. Since   H = .53 × G
3. Then   E = J + (.53 × G)
4. Since   J = 1.88 × K

and

5. Since   K = F − G

and

6. Since $J = 1.88 \times (F-G)$

7. Then $E = 1.88 \times (F - G) + (.53 \times G)$

                              $(1.88 \times G) - (.53 \times G) = (1.88 \times F) - E$

                              $1.35 \times G = (1.88 \times F) - E$

                              $G = [(1.88 \times F) - E)] / 1.35$

                              $G = [(1.88 \times 4.78) - 6.37] / 1.35$

                              $G = (8.9864 - 6.37) / 1.35 = 2.62/1.35 = 1.94$

                              $H = 1.94 \times .53 = 1.03$

8. Since $I = G - H$

                              $I = 1.94 - 1.03 = .91$ (Latent Earnings)

Quest for the Universal Valuation Model

Dean LeBaron, CFA

The subject of these proceedings is "Equity Markets and Valuation Methods." The other presentations have provided an excellent background on the history and the current perception of equity markets and valuation methods. I believe that the problem of which factors should be built into our portfolio models will be solved by studying the future from an international perspective. Therefore, I will try to define a global market for securities as it is arising now, and discuss the kinds of valuation models that may exist in the future.

The global market for securities is changing rapidly. Seventy-five percent of the world's investment markets are seeing their borders crumble. Many people thought that the U.S. dollar was a strong currency and that the country could produce everything it needed. We have now learned that the U.S. dollar is a weak currency, and that many of the things we need must be found elsewhere. Other countries have come to the same realization. The world's capital is moving about the world, and just as we have learned how to increase capital by raising money for junk bonds and the like, we must increase capital to move around the world's capital markets.

This movement is possible because of computers that can process data at an ever-increasing rate; the development of universal databases; and a universal valuation of securities. Essentially, a nonlocal market is being developed, in which securities are examined around the world using the same data and the same valuation model. Paul Aron described investment techniques being used successfully by the Japanese.[1] Much of the discussion on price/earnings ratios and accounting data would have seemed quite foreign to a Japanese investor 20 years ago, but not today.

[1] See Mr. Aron's presentation, pp. 71–77.

THE ERAS OF INVESTMENT

The quest to find the universal valuation model begins with a discussion of the evolution of U.S. market investors. In my view, there have been three distinct investment eras in the United States. The first era, 1945 to 1965, was dominated by individual investors. In the period following World War II, individual investors had a pocketful of savings. The supposedly inevitable postwar depression did not occur. Individuals wanted to spend their money on goods, but none were available. Instead, the money went into securities, and equities went up in a virtual straight line. Stocks were driven up on the basis of perfectly normal characteristics such as supply and demand and good news. Good news was a value component to those investors, much as the dividend discount model is to investors today. Name recognition was also important because individual investors had few data sources and analytical tools to help them evaluate unfamiliar companies. Pricing was not terribly important in that era, because investors could not calculate whether a stock was cheap or expensive based on the characteristics of good news and name recognition. Shareholder loyalty was very stable. Therefore, not surprisingly, some companies decided to print new issues to meet the increased demand for their shares.

The second era was dominated by institutions. It began in the mid-1960s and lasted approximately two decades, until 1985. It was a highly quantitative period. Institutional investors relied on their training in quantitative techniques to calculate precise stock valuations. They concentrated on buying low and selling high. The names of the stocks were irrelevant. The individual investor did not know how to do that; he bought high to sell higher. So everyone has experienced this rotational market characteristic called value-consciousness.

In its later years, the institutional market era

became quite speculative, as investors moved from one value characteristic or technique to another. Names were totally immaterial. All an investor needed to know was the CUSIP number and the covariance matrix. Now, this information may be replicated on floppy disks for $49.95.

Management control was not a factor in this era. Institutional investors have no intention of exercising management control. It is rather interesting that the difference between the price of control stock and noncontrol stock is about 4 percent in the United States, whereas it is about 200 percent in Europe. Institutions behave like agents rather than owners. Because of this, there are some anomalies and inefficiencies in the institutional market.

In my view, this second era has ended. We are now entering the corporate era. Institutions are declining in their relative importance in pricing securities. Another set of valuation characteristics is emerging. These characteristics are hard to define because there are no data or history to support them, but some clues may be found. First, corporations are taking charge of their own pricing of equity securities. No longer do corporate representatives go to analysts' lunches and say, "Please buy our security; we plan to increase our dividend next quarter." Rather, corporations buy their own stock if they think it is cheap, and sell it if they think it is expensive. The characteristics that corporate managements examine in valuing their own securities and those of other firms are quite different than those looked at by institutional investors. In fact, I doubt that a dividend discount model is used to value potential acquisition targets.

Control is important in the corporate era. Corporations examine their individual business units to see how they are doing and to determine whether the sum of the pieces equals the whole. They look at such things as the value of market share and the strategic location of assets. A different value is set on the entire enterprise when one has control. Unused debt capacity is valuable in a merger situation. Many of these factors are not specifically available in the Compustat database; institutional investors do not use them, because they cannot find them.

Companies today are run by financial people, not by sales people, as they were during the institutional era, or production people, as they were during the individual era. They are organized along product lines rather than regional lines. Strategic planning articles emphasize the importance of organizing along a global line, rather than a North American region, a European region, and so on. The global characteristics certainly lead one to the notion that increased liquidity will even out whatever differences there may be from one unit to another.

Corporations rely heavily on the increase in communications technology; one could not operate on a global basis without the communications capability available today. We are at the brink of computerized language translation, where even language barriers will become insignificant because we will be able to process foreign-language financial reports automatically. There is also an integrated monetary policy; the Japanese monetary authorities likely have more influence on American money supply these days than the Federal Reserve.

In a global climate it is impossible to regulate securities. There is no way to protect American investors when they wish to buy stocks in Japan, New Zealand, or London. Stock exchanges are going to become linked together. The corporate era relies on new global valuation characteristics, rather than the ones popular in the individual and institutional eras.

The North American markets have thus far been bound together by a common monetary climate, a common culture, and a highly integrated trade. The institutional investors who were so strong in the second era are losing ground to the corporate investors. The trend toward in-house money management has been in progress for more than a decade. Although institutional investors still write out the tickets, the major investment decisions are now being made by their clients. The corporate investor is taking back control of the funds for which they are responsible—and this represents a great deal of money. The corporate investor in North America has not gone global yet. They are dabbling in international securities in the old way, by picking stocks in local markets; it is not yet an integrated investment program.

Regulation will be an important factor in the new era of corporate investing. The transactions between corporate management and investment institutions are symptomatic of the changes. Management is now bribing institutions to give up control by offering a modest increase in dividends.

Each geographic and political region has a different relationship among investment institutions, corporate management, and the government. In Europe, there is a managed environment between institutions and corporations; they have developed a very clear alliance, frequently with government cooperation. That may well be part of the model for the future in the United States. By and large, Europe has a very corporate-controlled climate. Inside information—for your own purposes—is quite common; it provides confidence and is a way of cementing relationships. It becomes the currency by which these affiliations thrive. But, in reality, it is hard to determine what is inside information when everybody owns 21 percent of everybody else—everybody becomes an insider.

The Far East started out on an American model. General MacArthur wanted Japan to be a model version of his idea of America—not necessarily ours—and instituted systems which are compatible with ours. Culturally, many of these systems did not take root. In Japan, of course, they are quite accustomed to the use of leverage. They also use a portfolio approach to investing, rather than a stock-selection approach.

The most fascinating thing about Japanese investors is the information that they value. A recent study asked Japanese and American businessmen to rate a list of potential goals in order of importance. The list included such things as income, longevity, friendly relations with fellow workers, esteem, pride, reputation, and quality. The Japanese rated esteem as the number one goal and income as least important. The Americans rated income as the most important goal and esteem as the least important. I am not chauvinistic enough to say that my own notion of income maximization must be the primary goal of a Japanese investor; it seems perfectly clear that esteem can be just as important a valuation characteristic as income. Therefore, should we subject the Japanese to what a friend of mine used to refer to as "the tyranny of the price/earnings ratio," when they do not subscribe to that notion at all?

In a global model, Latin America may be the most attractive region now. It offers some potentially exciting real market opportunities. Emerging market funds are gaining popularity

and Latin America seems to be emerging from its dark ages. One particularly strong attribute is the region's lack of covariance with most of the other markets. The model of this region is close government and private control.

Again, as we begin to move toward a global market we will rely more and more on communications and technology. I have had two experiences with that issue recently. Computerized global trading has some interesting implications for the price per square foot on stock exchanges. To demonstrate that point, we set up the Batterymarch computerized trading system on top of a mountain in Switzerland and in Rio de Janiero. In both cases we were dealing with live activity using our computer in Boston which trades directly on the London and Paris markets. Our guests were intrigued by the potential.

The market will become integrated because of these communications capabilities. The databases are increasing; eventually they will be consolidated into one or two strong databases. Deregulation, which is now a worldwide phenomenon, will accelerate this process. Competitive markets, in turn, will increase the likelihood of this trend toward deregulation. Cross-trading facilitates integrated markets; for example, Sony is now traded in 18 markets. Equity prices will thrive in this climate, and be put to their best use.

The global market in this climate becomes countryless. Control is likely to be a major element, and currency will be dealt with as a separate characteristic.

Investors are probably interested in the risk-return characteristics of this global market. Perspective is the key. Investors must try to visualize their own location as being on a satellite when it comes to return expectations. For risk, on the other hand, one must adjust the return solutions to meet the conditions of the local community. The more flexibility there is in the system, the faster these things will happen and the sooner risk and return will blend together into a single parameter.

In my view, global investors are in our midst now, and have been for several years. They know, for example, that Americans will understand gold as a normal repository of value, and that the Japanese will learn to buy stocks on the dividend discount basis as this cross-cultural exchange takes place. The ultimate asset sheet in this global market will list all assets—common data for all—and have the flexibility to specify the currency mix of choice of the investor. The successful investor in this transitional phase is one who moves to the integrated standard first. Those who do not will give up profit because of their high-confidence, local-market biases. The profitable issuers will be listed in many markets; they will push for disclosure; they will consolidate control; they will use complex derivative instruments when profitable to issue; and most important, they will see the world as the smallest unit of financial market segmentation.

Question and Answer Session

QUESTION: Do you take into account earnings from financial market investments in your P/E adjustments?

ARON: Earnings are divided into two categories—operating and nonoperating earnings. Operating earnings obviously come from the operation of the main businesses, such as manufacturing plants. Nonoperating earnings (sometimes called financial earnings) are earnings that do not come from the operation of the plants. One element of non-operating earnings is the use of cash, which is not novel. There is a great deal of interest in financial earnings (also known as Zaitek), particularly since the earnings of a small chemical company named Tateho collapsed, entirely because of financial speculation. An article which appeared in *Barrons*[1] included a chart showing Zaitek profit as the major percentage of pretax profit for many corporations. I have a great deal of respect for Alan Abelson, so I tried to replicate the data; the numbers cited in *Barrons* seem to bear little or no relationship to the facts. Some companies have operated at a loss this past year; and therefore nonoperating earnings are the only earnings they could show. But in the companies appearing in *Barrons*, Zaitek earnings were overstated in seven cases, and understated in one case (see Appendix to this Question and Answer session). Two could not be verified because only part of the name of the companies appeared in the paper and too many companies have Mitsubishi and Sumitomo names. On average, in fiscal year 1986, operating earnings for 1,405 listed companies fell from 8,355 to 6,904 (million yen); interest and dividends received fell from 2,819 to 2,674 million yen (see Appendix to this question and answer session on p. 86).

So financial profits may be a big factor for some companies, but not for very many. By and large, nonoperating earnings did not increase significantly but rose as a percentage of the total because of operating earnings had declined. This is, in my opinion, just a temporary phenomenon.

[1] *Barrons*, September 7, 1987.

It is important to calculate operating expenses when considering operating earnings. The Zeitech profit shown in the Barron's article, for example, used gross not net operating earnings. The *Barrons* article was not complete.

QUESTION: If Japanese stocks are fairly priced now, were they formerly cheap, or have earnings or discount rates changed dramatically?

ARON: I am not sure that I know what "fairly priced" means, because the question still remains: What is the future of Japan? Price/earnings ratios, in my opinion, are merely a predictor of the future. The price/earnings ratio of Japan could be extremely low and if the outlook is one of gloom and doom, and then the price/earnings ratio is terribly overpriced; on the other hand, the price/earnings ratio could be very high and if the outlook is one of high growth, then the current ratio could be very underpriced. One must do more than just look at the numbers; one must look at the reality.

There is no question when I entered this business in 1969, Japanese earnings were extremely underpriced by American standards. For example, at that time, prices were single digit multiples and often no greater than the cash flow per share.

QUESTION: In your opinion, is Japanese urban real estate as fairly valued versus United States real estate as their stock market appears to be relative to the United States stock market?

ARON: Many Japanese companies have large holdings of land. Japan is going through a transformation now. Companies that own steel mills, textile mills, and printing houses were often located in urban areas, and they are redeveloping these areas. Sometimes the companies do the redevelopment themselves; sometimes they sell it. Some companies, Yasuda Fire, for example—a property and casualty company—is selling at 32 percent of its real book value. That is true for Sumitomo Marine as well. This is because these companies have enormous holdings in both land and securities valued at the lower of cost or market. The question is: Is the land overpriced? Is the land price going to come down? I do not pretend to be an expert on real estate. The situation is very simple. Japan is a country with half the population of the United States, occupying a territory smaller than California, of which 75 percent is noninhabitable (forests and mountains). Could you really expect land prices to be cheap?

QUESTION: Should we discard everything that we have learned about investments, or learn to apply it globally?

LeBARON: I think what we have learned does two things: First, it is useful for historical reasons, because it is a systematic way of looking at experiences that will relate to what we do in the future. Second, some of these things that we have had will remain in place because of our activities as agents. I wrote an article for the *Financial Analysts Journal* in which I said that you can look at the number anomalies or profit opportunities, and the most interesting ones you can describe are the ones that no one will do.[2] I think that is quite clear. Some of the anomalies that have been discussed in these proceedings cannot be implemented. For example, Batterymarch buys the yuck stocks—year in and year out. It is a nice, systematic way to make money. It is also a nice, systematic way of being an embarrassed manager and reducing your client base, which is why people do not do it. Buying unpopular stocks is not good for business, but it is good for rate of return. Prior to negiotiated commissions, I used to tell analysts when they called that I wanted to be their last call. I did not want to be the first. There was nobody competing for the last call, but I think it was the most profitable place to be, and I still do.

QUESTION: How much does Batterymarch have to know about a foreign stock before they are willing to hold it?

LeBARON: We know a lot about foreign stocks; we have stocks in different countries in a variety of different circumstances. We have been trying

for five years to develop a global firm located in one place. We do not want to have a variety of facilities—a London listening post, a Hong Kong listening post and so forth, because I think those would be barriers to understanding the common factors, rather than knowing more about the separate factors. So, for the degree to which we can look at Toyota, Volkswagen, General Motors on the same basis, I believe we know quite a bit. It is common in other countries' accounting conventions to hide earnings; it is common in U.S. accounting conventions to inflate them. I have greater faith in accounting conventions elsewhere.

QUESTION: What do you think of a strategy of identifying the best corporate managements on a global basis, then buying and holding their stocks?

LeBARON: Sounds like a great strategy to me— the notion of buy and hold is reasonably strong. We do not do that, because we think we can tilt the odds in our favor.

QUESTION: What will happen if the movement toward indexing approaches an extreme?

LeBARON: I think it has approached an extreme, and we will probably see a decline in indexing.

QUESTION: How do you reconcile the opening up of the securities markets with protectionism and defending local markets—new forces versus old provincial political biases?

LeBARON: Those are the things that could derail my forecast. If currency controls come on, world trade as a percentage of world GNP decreases, and protectionism occurs, then my forecast won't happen, or will happen much more slowly. At the moment, those factors seem to be a threat but not a reality because I think we are moving toward dropping those barriers. The present foreign currency exchange is a model for what the equity markets will look like in the future. But I recognize the characteristics that you describe; the political forces that argue for protectionism could stop it.

[2] LeBaron, Dean, "Reflections on Market Inefficiency", *Financial Analysts Journal*, (May/June) 1983, pp. 16-17, 23.

Appendix

Company	Zaitek Profits As a Percentage of Pre-Tax Profits According to Barron's Article %	Net Non Operating Income as a Percentage of Pre Tax Profits (Actual) %
Toyota	48	23
Nissan	107	71
Matsushita Electric	61	29
Matsushita	58	N/A
Sony	107	56
Sharp	81	58
Toa Nenryo	25	22
Sumitomo	46	N/A
Nippon Oil	106	101
Sanyo Electric	10	58

Sources: Barron's, Sept. 7, 1987.   Daiwa Securities Co. estimate.

Program Trading and Market Efficiency

Wayne H. Wagner

Today, there are more ways to accomplish investment goals and tailor investment solutions than ever before. Futures markets, passive products, portfolio insurance, and various arbitrage activities enable investment professionals to respond to individual investor needs. All of these activities may use program trading as a means of actuating the strategy.

Inventory, creativity, and broker agility have increased faster than the capacity of the exchange system to accommodate the supply/demand imbalances created by program trading. This is temporary: What appears today to be a market inefficiency will resolve into a market with greater efficiency.

WHAT IS PROGRAM TRADING?

Program trading is the trading of an aggregation of securities as though it were a single entity, simply because the investment manager *thinks* of it as an investment entity.

Program trading emerged in the mid 1970s when index fund managers began experimenting with portfolio-building methods that were more efficient than trading 500 stocks one by one.

Program trading is still used quite extensively by index funds, but it has turned out to be extremely useful in other applications as well. For example, when managers shift their style emphasis from one focus to another, a program trade may be used to execute the entire portfolio at once; alternatively, when a manager is terminated and a new manager is started, a program trade may be used to liquidate the existing portfolio and develop a new portfolio. The notoriety of program trading, however, arises from its use in hedging strategies involving futures and options.

The transition from an actively managed fund to an index fund illustrates some of the mechanics of program trading. Assume that an index fund manager receives a portfolio of 60 stocks from a terminated nonindex manager. The first step is to determine how much of the portfolio may be used in the index fund (ostensibly part of each of the 60 stocks), and then evaluate the remainder of the portfolio for its size, correlation, and ease of trading. The number of trading days it will take to liquidate the balance depends on the concentration in industries or individual stocks, whether there are illiquid stocks, and other factors which might make trading difficult. To liquidate the portfolio using program trading, this summary information will be given to a variety of brokers, who will be asked to bid on the package without knowing what is in it. It is a matter of trust and mutual respect to reveal the overall statistics of the contents of the package as accurately as possible, without revealing the names. After all, the manager must deal with the brokers in the future. The brokers are asked to bid on the package on a cents-per-share basis. The entire package goes to the lowest bidder.

Program trading is usually quite expensive, for two reasons. First, the broker knows the characteristics of the package, but not the names and quantities of the individual stocks. Second, if it is a one-sided trade, the broker may be at risk for the market movement, as well as for the movement in the individual securities. Elaborate systems have been built into the brokerage industry for handling these kinds of composite trades; but in general, the brokers will work these trades at their discretion, using their best skills.

At the end of the process, a reconciliation is performed. The differences between the stated strike prices and the actual trade prices on all the trades are tallied, and the broker's final commission is calculated. If the broker deserves extra money, the fund pays; if the broker was not able to deliver the securities at the promised closing prices, then he or she may have to pay the fund manager. I have seen checks in seven-digit figures paid by the broker to the fund.

The mechanics of program trading may be structured in a variety of ways. People have tried to use noon or open prices rather than closing prices. Broker incentive compensations have been offered. We have experimented with what we called "double-blind" programs—the brokers did not know what was in the package nor when we were going to strike it. In these cases, we let the broker pick a 15-minute window, and we chose the exact strike time within that 15-minute window. Program trading does not have to be done on a principal basis; it may be done on an agency basis, where it is hard to tell the difference between the program trade and a simple agency trade on one security. All of that is fairly routine.

Not all forms of program trading are so routine or well accepted in the markets as the index fund. With the development of the futures and index options markets, the ability to convert quickly from stocks to futures became a touchstone of a broker's trading prowess. This capability could be used, for example, by an index fund to garner extra returns by replacing the 500 individual stocks with the futures contract whenever the futures contract represented the cheapest way to own the index. Suppose an index fund sells a package of 500 securities—the S&P 500—and in exchange for that, it buys a futures contract on the S&P 500 in the same dollar amount. This type of trade is typically done when there is an arbitrage profit to be made. In these cases, the broker is usually guaranteeing the spread between the securities being sold and the futures contracts being bought. Because the same index is on both sides of the transaction, most of the risk is hedged. The only risk that the broker must be concerned with is that the futures contract and the underlying stocks may move in opposite directions, opening the gap between the cash and futures markets, which has not been accounted for.

Curiously, this new application significantly altered the goal of program trading: the original index fund traders were interested in low execution cost and were flexible about the timing of the trades. The futures swap, in contrast, was vitally concerned with the speed of execution; "legging" the transaction for more than a few minutes resulted in hazardous possibilities for the broker.

Program trading provides many benefits to investment managers, including speed of execution, ease of trading, and dealing with total trade expense as a single item rather than a sum of difficult-to-measure parts. Most importantly, it frees the manager to conceptualize investment products in terms of strategies rather than individual stocks.

LIQUIDITY—WHATEVER THE FAIR PRICE

Program trading, by definition, involves the simultaneous trading of a large number of stocks. Because of this characteristic, the supply/demand balance of individual stocks is ignored. Program trading also transfers both a time-intensive workload and trading risk to the broker. As a result, program trades are more costly to service than other trading techniques.

Because program trading is so easy to use, it may be applied in situations where it is not appropriate—where the benefits are neither relevant nor necessary. All too easily, the medium becomes the message. Just because it is easier to trade does not mean that it has become more profitable to trade. Liquidity is not a free good—as evidenced by the elaborate facilities and extensive capital that exist on Wall Street to create liquidity.

This cost may be higher than the value received. Many people believe that active manager underperformance implies that institutional managers trade too much and are inefficient users—actually overusers—of apparent information concerning the value of companies.

In addition, program trading (and the strategies that apply the technique) creates traders who are indifferent to company "value," that specie which current exchanges are designed to equilibrate. As a result, recent markets have been subjected to both higher levels and a faster tempo of supply/demand balance; the exchange system is still adapting to this new style of trader.

WHAT IS MARKET EFFICIENCY?

There are many possible definitions of market efficiency. Market efficiency is a subject dear to the hearts of regulators, market economists, and the defenders of a capitalist society. Yet all of these parties operate under different definitions, adopting the ones that are most applicable in their realm.

First, the regulators: The SEC seems to insist on a "level playing field" concept of efficiency; i.e., no one is allowed to profit through misappropriation of information that arises from privileged access. The exchanges tend to equate narrow spread with market efficiency, a definition which seems as appropriate to "liquidity" as efficiency. As we look upon it, the question of efficiency is "What does this liquidity cost, and are the costs worth paying?"

Turning to the theorists, the random walk market economists emphasize the idea that information is quickly and correctly imbedded in the price. The test is whether autoserial correlation is found in price series. If autoserial correlation is present, estimates of the next period's price may be improved by knowing recent prices. While most studies have found zero autoserial correlation in individual stocks, there definitely is autoserial correlation in the indexes, caused by nonsimultaneous trading of issues that comprise the index. This is inefficient: market-wide information which impacts all stocks, yet affects different prices at different times. For this reason the futures contract, not the index, is the best instantaneous measure of the market.

In the stock market, the market factor common to all stocks gets imbedded in the prices of some individual stocks faster than others. Thus, the futures market seems an enhancement to market efficiency because all stocks can be traded faster.

EFFICIENT CAPITAL FORMATION

Securities markets unattached to economic reality may surely be called inefficient. If valid economic objectives are not enhanced by activities that use program trading, those markets are surely inefficient because capital invested in those markets is being diverted from more productive uses. Fortunately, redeeming social value in the futures market is easy to see:

- Hedgers may take risks they otherwise could not tolerate, thus making their capital available for equity investment.
- Market functionaries lay off risk, thus improving liquidity at low cost.
- Finally, the futures market is closely connected with the stock market. When a futures position is opened, the likely other side of the trade is a market functionary. Market functionaries are survivors: they lay off residual risk by reversing the futures trade in the stock market. Thus, net demand for futures shifts quickly into net demand for stocks and provides the grist for efficient allocation of capital.

Program traders are concerned solely with the *aggregate* aspects of the trade entity, however. They invest proportionately in all constituents of the aggregate, inefficient firms as well as those that make good use of capital. Which raises the question: Who is minding the store, making sure that a functioning pricing mechanism exists to assure proper allocation of capital?

Program traders care very little about what is going on in an individual company. They will invest proportionately in anything. These funds are flowing not only to the good users of capital, but also to the inefficient companies, and those who cannot offer a competitive rate of return on their capital. In a sense, futures traders, index funds, and other passive investors rely on a pricing mechanism that they do not support very strongly. That pricing mechanism is, in effect, provided by others; however, that was always true. Most orders do not establish prices; they are matching an equal number of shares—purchases with sales. It really does not matter that those shares traded, regardless of how large the volume is. It is only an imbalance between the buys and the sells that causes a change in the price and leads to the correct price of a security, whether a program trader is involved or not. More importantly, program trading does nothing that removes the incentive for the creation and discovery of value; as long as there is one investor who thinks the stock price is too high or too low, that investor will act to capture the value of that information.

These types of problems are self-correcting: if any inefficiencies materialize, someone will appear to increase his—or his client's—fortune.

VOLATILITY OR VELOCITY?

Many studies have shown that market variances have not increased as a result of program trading, yet there clearly is a widespread perception to the contrary. Perhaps it is the velocity that has increased, rather than the volatility: when prices have a reason to be higher or lower, program trading has increased the speed at which prices adjust.

If this is a problem, it appears to be more of a mechanical than an economic problem. The tempo of the order-processing capacity needed to maintain an orderly market seems to have temporarily fallen behind. Market players who are insensitive to individual company value and supply/demand pressures create a need for new market structures which have yet to evolve.

This is not a new problem. Many exchange mechanisms have evolved in the past to handle supply/demand imbalances. Call markets, delayed openings, secondary offerings, sunshine trades, and the normal day-to-day give and take that is part of the exchange floor culture all exist to equilibrate supply and demand.

The recent SEC proposal to halt trading across the board seems overly drastic, yet it is consistent with tried-and-true methods that balance supply and demand. I do not feel that such draconian measures are necessary: the markets will adjust to the mindset of the program trader, and as they do, the velocity will become an insignificant problem. In the meantime, it would be a foolish trader indeed who did not keep an eye on the S&P spread!

SUMMARY

Program trades exist because they facilitate investment solutions that satisfy investor needs. We now have far more powerful tools to tailor-make investment outcomes and better accomplish investment goals: the "investment results factory" has become more efficient.

It serves us well to remember that the objective of pension investment is to accumulate funds to pay pension benefits. If program trading increases the probability of fulfilling the pension promise or reduces the cost of providing pension benefits—or both—then investors, managers, and markets have become more efficient in fulfilling the main objective of pension investment.

Valuation of Convertibles

Michael L. McCowin, CFA

Convertible securities have the attributes of both equity and fixed-income instruments. It is somewhat like being the child of a mixed marriage. More often than not, however, the equity side is the dominant partner in that marriage because most managers, plan sponsors, and consultants would allocate their convertibles as equity, if forced to choose between the two. That is a carry-over from the days when managers used convertibles to slide stocks in the back door when they could not get past their plan sponsor's specified equity limits. But at last, the child of this mixed marriage is growing up and has an identity of its own.

The convertible market is expanding. Corporate plan sponsors are now specifically allocating a portion of their plan assets to convertibles. Interestingly, many of the same plan sponsors are simultaneously issuing convertibles. The convertible market is no longer composed only of third-tier companies who cannot raise money any other way. Consultants are now tracking convertible managers, and the industry is trying to find a suitable index to measure them against.

Some people argue that convertibles are *not* a separate asset class, but are equity derivatives; and they do, of course, derive some of their value from their potential for participation in common stock price appreciation. But they also derive a significant amount of their value from their fixed-income qualities. Therefore, I believe it is appropriate to treat convertibles as a separate asset class.

Convertibles are special; they represent a uniquely attractive asset. Just as a child will inherit traits from both parents, so a convertible will inherit traits from each of its parents; and just as you would never try to forecast the physical characteristics or behavior of a child on the basis of just one parent, so it would be foolhardy to try to forecast the behavior of a convertible solely on the basis of what might happen to the common stock. Yet most of the literature focuses almost entirely on the equity characteristics of convertibles. The heavy emphasis on break-even time and other equity-oriented measures in the literature reflect a carry-over from the days when convertibles were considered "back door" equities. Fortunately, this is changing.

ATTRACTIVE QUALITIES OF CONVERTIBLES

Let me begin by explaining why convertibles are uniquely attractive. Figure 1 depicts the behavior of a convertible portfolio relative to stock and bond portfolios. During a period of rising security prices, as shown on the right, a stock portfolio will typically rise more rapidly than a bond portfolio. In this environment, convertibles tend to rise more rapidly than bonds, but less rapidly than stocks. Last year was a good example of that phenomenon, with a strong stock market and a weak bond market. As of the beginning of September 1987, most convertible portfolios were up about 20 percent, with the stock market up 35 percent and bonds flat. In a period of declining prices, the bond-like quality of the convertibles comes into play and tends to cushion the downside, so that prices will not decline as rapidly as the common stocks, but more rapidly than a simple bond portfolio. Consequently, convertibles have a nonlinear expected return distribution. This nonlinearity may be the single most important attribute of convertible securities, and it is something that is inherent in the security itself. It does not require any overt action or decision by a portfolio manager. In addition, the favorable bending of that return distribution may, at times, permit a convertible portfolio to outperform a balanced mix of stocks and bonds and, in some cases, even stocks alone.

In comparing a convertible portfolio to a mix of stocks and bonds, keep in mind that the stock/bond mix would have to be adjusted continuously, whereas with the convertible portfolio, this occurs automatically. This adjustment is also issue-specific. If a particular stock goes down or up, the security will respond specifi-

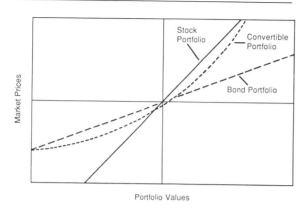

Source: Harris Investment Management

FIGURE 2. Convertible Bond Price Response Curve

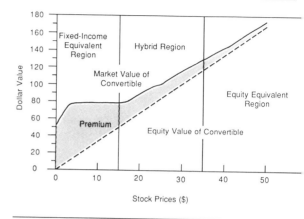

Source: Harris Investment Management

cally to that stock. Given this attractive bending of the return profile, one might expect that returns on convertibles would be surprisingly good, and they are. In fact, in certain market environments, it is possible for convertibles to outperform stocks, with somewhat less volatility.

Table 1 presents a comparison of monthly returns from a convertible portfolio, a bond index, and a stock index. The table illustrates the monthly mean return and standard deviation of return over four holding periods: one year, three years, five years, and ten years. Notice in the five-year and ten-year periods, the convertible portfolio earned 15 to 20 basis points more than the S&P 500 on a monthly basis, and

had a lower standard deviation of return. In this case, low volatility is not a function of poor pricing, although pricing is a problem with convertibles. The pricing process in this convertible fund is rigorous and well-audited. About five years ago, Harris Trust created a convertible index against which to measure the portfolio manager, believing that a 50/50 mix of stocks and bonds was too easy a benchmark. The convertible index was priced on a monthly basis for five years. Over the five-year period, the monthly mean return is slightly less than the S&P 500, and the volatility is considerably less. So low volatility appears to be a function of the instrument itself.

Most convertibles may be put into one of three categories: fixed-income equivalent, hybrids, or common stock equivalents. We find this framework useful because the behavior of the security is different in each category. In addition, the opportunity to exploit the return distribution and the valuation parameters that one would want to emphasize in any modeling approach tend to vary across categories.

The price of a convertible is related to the value of the underlying common stock price. Figure 2 shows the price behavior of a typical convertible security relative to the underlying common stock price, assuming that interest rates are unchanged. Every convertible may be exchanged for some number of shares of common stock; that number of shares is called the conversion ratio. The conversion value—or equity value—of the convertible is calculated by

TABLE 1.   Risk Versus Reward

	Harris Convertible Fund	Shearson/ Lehman Master	S&P 500*
1-Year Geometric Mean	1.96	1.18	1.43
Standard Deviation	2.97	1.50	5.28
3-Year Geometric Mean	1.34	1.45	1.42
Standard Deviation	2.75	1.87	4.25
5-Year Geometric Mean	1.74	1.36	1.52
Standard Deviation	3.35	2.30	4.22
10-Year Geometric Mean	1.25	0.80	1.09
Standard Deviation	3.80	2.30	4.24

*Including income. All figures are shown on a *monthly* basis. Periods ending December 31, 1986.
Source: Harris Investment Management

multiplying the price of the common stock by the conversion ratio. The result is a linear relationship, represented in the figure by the broken line.

As the common stock price moves up, the market value of the convertible moves up with it. At a relatively high stock price, the behavior of the common stock totally dominates the movement of the convertible, and the premium is considerably reduced. When the conversion premium drops below 10 or 15 percent, and the stock price movement tends to be dominant, the convertible is classified as an equity equivalent. As the common stock price drops, the bond characteristic becomes dominant and the premium increases. As the premium gets larger, the price of the convertible becomes less sensitive to the price of the underlying common stock, and more sensitive to changes in interest rates. Typically, when the premium is greater than 35 or 40 percent and the convertible is trading at 20 or 25 percent over its straight bond value, the convertible is classified as a fixed-income equivalent. These are also called "busted" convertibles, and are often treated as junk bonds.

Convertibles in the middle are classified as hybrids. The hybrids have three important characteristics: (1) they respond to both common stock price changes and to interest-rate movements; (2) they get the maximum benefit of the bent-return effect; and (3) the valuation process is trickiest in the middle range.

There are many factors that affect the behavior of convertible prices. The price of the stock, interest-rate movements, the maturity of the underlying bond—or convertible preferred stock, if it has a maturity—and the conversion ratio are all very important factors. Typically, the maturity and conversion ratio are set at the time of issue and do not change. The coupon level on the bond and the dividend level of the stock are quite important because they determine the income-pickup relationship for the convertible—noting, of course, that the coupon is normally constant, whereas the dividend may change. The issue size is important because it affects both liquidity and whether certain institutional players will be involved in the issue. General market conditions may also affect pricing. Finally, the call provision and the volatility of the underlying common stock are perhaps the most important factors.

The effects of these factors vary depending on the security. In the equity-equivalent category, the common stock price is very important and interest rates are not terribly important for convertibles. It is just the opposite for the debt-equivalent category: interest rates are very important and common stock price changes are less important. On the equity-equivalent side, the call provisions become quite critical, and the maturity and credit quality of the bond may be of fairly little importance. On the bond side, call provisions—certainly call provisions that are tied to stock price levels—are quite unimportant; and maturity and credit quality may be far more important. All of these factors are somewhat important for convertibles in the hybrid category. Thus, the relevant valuation factors and how they are weighted is partly a function of the type of convertible.

All discussions of convertibles include the concept of break-even time or pay-back period—the time it takes the buyer to recover the premium paid for the convertible. I believe this concept is slightly overemphasized. The literature provides several different ways to compute break-even time, but not all of them make sense. The least objectionable and most widely used method is the "equal-dollar" method, which assumes an equal dollar amount invested in either the stock or the convertible. But even that formula ignores the time value of money; it treats the income picked up in the third or fourth year the same as the income picked up in the first year.

In preparing a paper for the ICFA on valuing convertible securities, Luke Knecht and I provided a formula for calculating the break-even time which incorporates the time value of money (Knecht and McCowin, 1987). The method treats break-even as a process for repaying a loan. The amount of the loan represents the value of the additional shares that would be needed to equate a convertible purchase with an equal dollar amount of the underlying stock. When the interest rate on the loan is zero, this formula gives the same break-even time as the traditional equal-dollar method. As the interest rate increases, however, the break-even time gets longer. We have dubbed it the "loan-repayment" method of break-even time. The formula appears in Table 2.

CONVERTIBLE VALUATION METHODS

Convertible valuation methods may be grouped into three broad types. The first type involves simple rules of thumb. Examples of such rules include "The break-even time must be less than the time to the first call, so that I can get my premium back before they can call it"; and "I never buy a convertible with a premium of more than 25 percent." Such rules may sometimes be helpful guides; but used in isolation, they may also be very misleading. The second type of valuation method is the subjective model. This method typically involves making a subjective forecast of stock price or interest rate movements, or both, and then a subjective judgment of how the convertible would likely be priced, based on that forecast. Again, it is a useful idea; but the outcome may be overly influenced by the subjective input. Finally, the third type is the quantitative model. This method does not depend on subjective forecasts of stock prices or interest rates. I will describe one such model shortly, but first I would like to comment on another aspect of convertible valuation.

The strategic *perspective* of convertible investors must also be considered. There are convertible specialists who manage only convertibles. There are risk-averse equity managers who want a measure of protection and who are willing to pay the convertible premium to get it. There are also income-oriented equity managers who use convertibles to develop more income—for example, personal trust managers who cannot buy non-dividend-paying stocks. Then there are the fixed-income managers—the insurance companies and junk bond managers—and last, a lot of hedge funds and arbitrage specialists that deal in convertible securities.

Each of these players emphasizes different factors when evaluating a convertible. For example, risk-averse equity managers or the income-oriented manager might place great emphasis on how much yield pick-up there is, and what the break-even time might be. They would tend to be far more active in the equity-equivalent end of the spectrum. Bond managers, on the other hand, may be rather indifferent to break-even time. Instead, they may be interested in the premium over the straight bond value, not over the equity value. A very high premium over the equity value, which would

really turn off an equity manager, might be quite unimportant to a bond manager. The strategic perspectives vary; if one investor is selling and another is buying at a given price, it does not necessarily mean that either one is wrong, even though each may feel, based on his own strategic perspective, that he may have gotten the better side of the bargain.

THE HARRIS CONVERTIBLE VALUATION MODEL

I would like to describe the convertible valuation model used at Harris Investment Management to illustrate the key valuation issues, and present some examples of its use. I will then discuss the model's limitations.

The essence of the Harris approach is to treat each convertible as a combination of a bond and a warrant, which, of course, is exactly what it is. (It may be noted that unit offerings of notes and warrants behave exactly the same as convertibles, provided the note may be used at par to exercise the warrant.) The first step, then, is to determine the value of a straight debt instrument of comparable maturity and coupon for the particular issuer involved. This is simply a matter of deciding how many basis points should be added to the risk-free rate, and then computing the price that will equate the coupon and the maturity of the instrument for the required rate. The formula is shown in Table 2. This formula does not allow for sinking fund payments, but it satisfies our needs.

TABLE 2. Valuation methods: Formulas

A. Break-even or Payback Period: Loan Repayment Method

$$N = [\ln(x) - \ln(x-i)]/\ln(1+i);$$

where i is the annual interest rate expressed as a decimal and x is the ratio of the annual repayment to the original loan balance; ln is the natural logarithm.

B. Bond plus warrant approach
calculation of investment (bond) value, IV:

$$IV = (.5C/Y) + [(1/(1+Y)^t) * (100-(.5C/Y))]$$

where:

IV = Investment value or market value (price) of the bond per 100 face amount

C = Coupon rate in dollars per 100 face amount

Y = Yield to maturity as a % per semi-annual period

T = Number of semiannual periods to maturity

Source: Luke Knecht and Michael McCowin

The second step is to calculate the value of the warrant feature embedded in the convertible. A number of models use the Black-Scholes [1973] framework to compute the warrant value. Unfortunately, this method assumes non-callable warrants, whereas virtually all convertibles are callable. Luckily, a binomial solution for valuing warrant features was developed by Cox, Ross, and Rubinstein [1979].

Figure 3 illustrates the Cox, Ross, and Rubinstein approach. The example is based on a common stock with a starting price of $25 per share and a convertible issued with a conversion price that is 25 percent higher, or $31.25. In addition, it is assumed that the convertible is issued with the following provision: If the common stock price becomes 40 percent higher than the $31.25 conversion price (which would be $43.75), the bond can be called. Barring that, it is callable after five years. The example assumes a volatility of 0.20. In essence, this method of determining the value of a warrant uses a tree of future stock prices to calculate an expected value, which is then discounted back to the present. The tree propagates future stock prices, with the probability of moving up or down from any given node being equal. In the absence of any call provisions, the solution is a log-normal distribution of future prices.

This approach can accommodate early redemption features. To incorporate the call provisions, this process is truncated at a specified price level. In this example, it is assumed that the bond becomes callable after five years, or if the stock price rises to $43.75. Thus, when the price passes through the $43.75 level, that node is no longer allowed to propagate.

Similarly, after five years at node T-5, the bond becomes callable. This model assumes that the issuer would call the bond only to force conversion. Normally, there is a provision requiring 20 or 30 days between when it is called and when it is redeemed, so the company will want to be sure that the stock price will not drop below the call price in the interim; otherwise the company would have to redeem in cash rather than forcing conversion. Thus, there is usually a buffer between the conversion price and likely

FIGURE 3. Binomial Option Tree

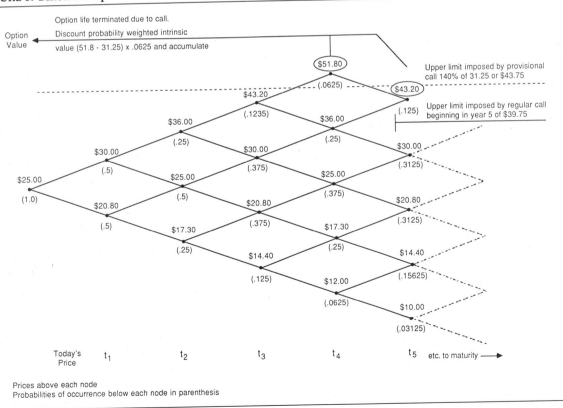

Source: Harris Investment Management

call price. In this case, we have assumed that it will be called at $39.75. That is approximately 27 percent above the conversion price. This might be a little high for a stock with a volatility of 0.20; it is more reasonable for a more volatile stock. In any event, the model assumes that after five years, the bond will be called when the stock price reaches $39.75.

There is one additional step in the valuation process. Using the same example, suppose the common stock rises to $50, and the straight bond value was calculated at $81. At this price, the convertible is in the money and the bond can be used at par in the exercise of this warrant; this is in essence a put on the bond at par. In this case, the put feature must also be valued. Thus, the sum of the straight bond value, the value of the warrant, and the value of the put make up the value of a convertible bond.

VALUING CONVERTIBLES: SOME EXAMPLES

I would like to present two examples to illustrate the valuation model and evaluate the efficiency of the convertible market. One example deals with sensitivity of convertibles to common stock price changes, and the other to interest-rate changes. Both of these examples are based on actual transactions; the transaction costs are included.

The first example is based on Hercules 8 percent convertible bonds. In the spring of 1986, the common stock appeared to be undervalued; but, of course, the convertible model does not know anything about that. It assumes that the stock price is equally likely to move up or down. We were pleased to find that the convertible also appeared to be undervalued, giving us our favorite type of convertible security: undervalued convertible, undervalued common stock.

Table 3 presents the important valuation assumptions and the model results. The risk-free rate was 8 percent at that time. We assumed a 120 basis points yield premium for the Hercules credit. The bond is callable on August 15, 1988 at a price of $105.60. There is no provisional call on this bond. The conversion price is $44.70. The stock was yielding 3.5 percent and the volatility was 0.27. The price of the convertible on March 14 was $119.25.

The table also provides the theoretical value of the convertible. The model indicated that the value of a comparable straight debt instrument was $88.40; the option value was $35.38—$15.82 per share times the conversion ratio of 2.236. Thus, the package was worth approximately $123.75, approximately 4 percent more than its current price.

The lower half of the table shows the analysis two months later. Interest rates had dropped 60 basis points, so the bond value had increased from $88.40 to $93.93. The stock price had moved up to $47.25. The convertible had moved up 9 points, from $119.25 to $128.25 about a 7.5 percent increase. Running the new information through the model generated a new theoretical value for the package of $126.39. Thus, the convertible was now overvalued.

The second example deals with the effect of interest rates and efficiency. This example is

---

TABLE 3.   Convertible Valuation: Hercules Example

Valuation of Hercules 8% of August 15, 2010
Callable 8/15/88 @$105.60; No provisional call
Conversion price $44.70

As of March 14, 1986:

Risk-free rate 8%; Yield premium 1.2%	
Common yield 3.5%; Volatility .27	
Convertible bond price $119¼	
Stock Price $46	
Theoretical Value:	
Bond value	$ 88.40
Option value	35.38
Package	$123.78
Value/price	103.8%
Option value/share	$ 15.82

As of May 14, 1986:

Risk-free rate 7.4%; Yield premium 1.2%	
Common yield 3.4%; Volatility .27	
Convertible bond price $128¼	
Stock price $47¼	
Theoretical Value:	
Bond value	$ 93.93
Option value	32.46
Package	$126.39
Value/price	98.5%
Option value/share	$ 14.51

Source: Harris Investment Management

TABLE 4. IBM—Common vs. Convertible Bond

	March 3, 1987	April 3, 1987
Stock Price	$138⅜	$148⅝
Bond Price	118⅛	122.4
Yield Advantage	3.5%	3.5%
Premium	31.2%	26.6%
Break-Even Time	9.9 yr.	8.6 yr.
Theoretical Convertible Value	$118.50	$118.00
Value/Price	100.3%	96.4%
Risk-Free Rate	7.45%	8.25%
Inv. Value of Bond	$ 97.70	$ 90.80
Warrant Value of Bond	20.80	27.20

Source: Harris Investment Management

based on the IBM 7.875 percent of November 21, 2004 convertible debenture. If there is going to be an efficient issue, this should be it, because of the size ($1.2 billion) and quality (AAA) of the issue. One type of inefficiency is a lag between what happens to the price of the convertible and what happens to the price of the common stock or to interest rates. The lag tends to be slightly more pronounced with interest-rate changes, but it also occurs commonly with respect to common stock price changes.

Table 4 shows a comparison between IBM stock and the IBM convertible bond on two dates in the spring of 1987. In March, the convertible appeared fairly priced; in April it appeared overvalued. What happened? The stock had moved up 10 points, and the bond had moved up 4.50 points, which seems intuitively logical; and the premium had declined slightly, which seemed normal. The theoretical value of the convertible, however, was unchanged. The missing part, of course, was what had happened to interest rates. The stock had certainly moved up and the warrant value in the bond had increased by 6.50 points, but the bond market took quite a big hit between the first of March and the middle of April, so the value of the straight-debt had declined by about 7 points. Clearly, the market had incorporated changes in the common stock value, but it had not picked up all of what had happened to the underlying bond value.

At this point, one might think that the convertible market is not efficient with respect to interest-rate changes, but is with respect to common stock price changes. It turns out that is

not true, either. Table 5 presents the model valuation data for April 13, 1987 and April 15, 1987. Keep in mind that this issue has a market value of $1.5 billion; it is listed; and it is actively traded on a daily basis by many major firms. Competitive bids on IBM convertible bonds will come back pennies apart—so certainly it is trading efficiently. So the question is whether there is valuation efficiency.

On April 13, the model indicated that the convertible was 3.5 percent overpriced, based on the fact that the risk-free rate was 8.25 percent, the bond was $122.40, and the stock was $148.625. Two days later, these bonds were theoretically undervalued. The same bonds which could be sold for $122.40 on April 13 could be purchased for $121 on April 15, even though the common stock price was $2.375 higher and interest rates had not changed! Was this an anomaly? I do not know. Perhaps it was

---

TABLE 5. Convertible Valuation: IBM Example

Valuation of IBM 7⅞% of November 21, 2004
Callable 11/21/88 @$104.725; No provisional call
Conversion price $153.66

As of April 13, 1987:

Risk-free rate 8¼%; yield premium 0.67%
Common yield 3.0%; Volatility .26
Convertible bond price $122.4
Stock price $148⅝

Theoretical Value:	
Bond Value	$ 90.80
Option value	27.20
Package	$118.00
Value/price	96.4%
Option value/share	$ 41.74

As of April 15, 1987:

Risk-free rate 8¼; Yield premium 0.67%
Common yield 2.9%; Volatility .26
Convertible bond price $121
Stock price $151

Theoretical Value:	
Bond value	$ 90.80
Option value	39.00
Package	$129.80
Value/price	107.3%
Option value/share	$ 59.90

Source: Harris Investment Management

a delayed reaction to the earlier interest-rate changes. In any event, it is not an isolated case.

CONVERTIBLE MODELS: SOME LIMITATIONS

Any convertible model will, of course, have limitations. One specific limitation of the Harris model is that it does not allow for calls intended to redeem the bond. Until recently that was a rare occurrence; however, many convertibles were issued with double-digit coupons several years ago and are now being refinanced at lower interest rates. Another problem is that the model does not specifically incorporate interest-rate changes, nor does it incorporate changes in the yield curve over time. It is primarily a common stock factor model. Also, the model always assumes usability of the note, and that is not always the case. If the convertible has a note that is not usable, the model must be adjusted.

Convertibles are complex instruments. Some convertibles are being issued with put features—usually it is a put feature on the bond; sometimes it is even a put on the stock. There are reset features—sometimes resetting the conversion ratio, sometimes resetting the coupon; there are Eurodollar convertibles (Euros), which only pay their coupons annually. That may not seem very important, but for the investors who owned Texaco convertibles, which paid an 11.875 coupon annually in May when they filed for bankruptcy in mid-April, the difference between an annual coupon and a semiannual coupon was quite significant. It put $250 million in Texaco's coffers. There are also provisions which may deny convertible owners the final coupon when the provisional call kicks in.

The CALFED Eurodollar convertible is an interesting example of a bond with a special feature. It has a put provision that allows the owner of the convertible to put the bond back to the company at $123 in February of 1993. This requires a modification to the valuation model,

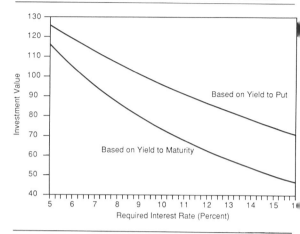

FIGURE 4. Investment Value vs. Required Rate: CALFED 6.5% Eurodollar Convertible

Source: Harris Investment Management

but all we do is compute the investment value based on both yield-to-maturity and yield-to-put; and for any given level of interest rates, the difference is a proxy for the value of the additional put, and thus can be added to the model's valuation estimate. Figure 4 illustrates the investment value versus the yield on the CALFED example.

CONCLUSION

In conclusion, I will reiterate three points. First, convertible securities are indeed a separate and very attractive asset class, and deserve to be dealt with as such. It is a very dynamic market. Billions of dollars can come and go in this market overnight. Second, in valuing convertibles, do not ignore the strategic perspective of individual investors. Different objectives and different strategies may result in different perceptions of value. Finally, I feel that some sort of quantitative model is absolutely indispensable in evaluating convertible securities. It should be noted, however, that there will never be a model that covers all of the features of all convertibles.

Question and Answer Session

QUESTION: How does portfolio insurance fit into the program-trading framework? Does it exacerbate or reduce market inefficiencies?

WAGNER: Program trading involves the desire to trade rapidly without respect to the underlying value of the securities, and so it does exacerbate the problem of market inefficiencies.

QUESTION: Will program trading work for a package of securities in the over-the-counter markets or smaller foreign markets? If so, will this increase the liquidity of these markets and open them to greater institutional penetration?

WAGNER: It is hard for me to see how program trading will increase the liquidity of any market, because it is a series of demands for stocks irrespective of the existing supply and demand. There have been program trades for as many as 3,000 securities. I know they have been used in the international market, although it is alleged to be a nightmare—not so much because of the program trade, but because of the foreign brokers and exchanges.

QUESTION: What is the expected transaction cost on one day's volume of each of 50 stocks in a diversified program of stocks?

WAGNER: The amount moves around a lot. We did a lot of packaged trading on a blind-blind basis three-and-a-half years ago. In these cases, we removed the market risk by moving a balanced program of $100 million of buys and $100 million of sells. In general, we moved approximately 50 sells and 200 buys in a day. We limited it to a quarter-day's trading volume in each stock. At that time, the winning bid was a low of $.09 per share, and the most we ever paid was $.195 per share. Because this was constructed in such a way that it would be difficult to manipulate the strike prices—because we did not know when we were striking it—we thought that that was a pretty good approximation of the total transaction cost.

QUESTION: Is there a maximum dollar amount at which most brokerage firms will either refuse to bid, or bid so high as to effectively eliminate your interest in them?

WAGNER: If that limit exists, I don't know of it.

QUESTION: Has program trading shortened the market's time horizon?

WAGNER: Certainly transaction levels have gone up across the board, but I do not think that it has shortened pension fund advisors' horizon with respect to investment management. But it has made the market move faster to where it is going.

QUESTION: What are the pros and cons of selling options against convertible positions?

McCOWIN: We have not used options, so I cannot discuss the pros and cons. Part of the reason for not using options is that we would just as soon not have convertibles with puts, although the Europeans seem to love them. We feel that we are in the business of taking risk, so we do not want a built-in defense mechanism. Sally Mae came out with a bond that had a put in it which was separable, and that was fine—you can trade it. But in most cases you cannot realize both values. If you have a put and a call, you are either going to put the bond or call the stock, but you cannot have them both.

QUESTION: With the binomial model, the accuracy depends on the number of nodes and the unit of time. How many nodes and what unit of time do you use?

McCOWIN: We use quarters in our model, and at least 50 nodes, or it would not be useful. We assume 30-year maturities for the convertible preferreds that do not have maturities. So, if there are 30 years, to do something more often than quarterly gets tough.

QUESTION: Given the small size of the market, aren't convertible managers really managing a lot of junk? If so, is the Goldman 100, which is a relatively high-quality index, an appropriate index for convertibles?

McCOWIN: The only problem with the Goldman 100, aside from the fact that there are only 100 issues, is that they do not want to tinker with it. Gresham's law works here: the good guys go away; the stock runs up and they disappear. The bad guys live forever. If you build that kind of an index, it will have a bias towards junk. I think the index problem is very serious; every index you look at will have a problem. I do not have anything against the Goldman Index, but it does have that bias in it.

QUESTION: Has the increased correlation of stock and bond returns over the past 10 years reduced much of the "hedge value" of convertible securities? If stocks decline and so do bonds, where is the floor?

McCOWIN: I do not know if I agree with the assumption of increased correlation between stock and bond returns. In fact, the more stock and bond markets diverge, the more value convertibles should have—in theory. The more they move in sync, the less convertibles will benefit from this process.

QUESTION: Some analysts have stated that convertibles are underpriced. If that is so, why should corporations issue them?

McCOWIN: It is one thing to say that they are underpriced and another thing to say that they have an attractive return profile. Actually, we are finding that more and more often, our model indicates that convertibles are overvalued rather than undervalued. Corporations issue convertibles because it has been in vogue, ever since IBM and Westinghouse did it. It is almost like the portfolio managers who never wanted to talk about convertibles because they only bought stocks that went up; and if you only buy stocks that go up, you are never going to need convertibles as a portfolio manager. Corporations think that they are selling you their stock at a premium and getting a cheaper rate on debt. They think there is a little bit of a free lunch. Frankly, I don't think they do much more valuation on it than that.

Reference List

Arnott, R.D. 1983. What hath MPT wrought: Which risks reap rewards? *Journal of Portfolio Management* 10 (Fall): 5-11.

Aron, P.H. 1981. Report No. 24, *Are Japanese P/E Multiples Too High? Some Preliminary and Tentative Observations and Thoughts.* New York: Daiwa Securities America, Inc.

Aron, P.H. 1984. Report No. 27, *Japanese Price Earnings Multiples Revisited: Some Further But Still Tentative Observations and Thoughts.* New York: Daiwa Securities America, Inc.

Aron, P.H. 1986. Report No. 29, *Japanese Price Earnings Multiples: An Update.* New York: Daiwa Securities America, Inc.

Aron, P.H. 1987. Report No. 30, *Japanese Price Earnings Multiples: Refined and Updated.* New York: Daiwa Securities America, Inc.

Aron, P.H. 1987. Report No. 31, *Japanese Price Earnings Multiples: Updated as of August 31, 1987.* New York: Daiwa Securities America, Inc.

Bachelier, L. 1900. *Theory of Speculation.*

Banz, R.W. 1981. The relationship between return and market value of common stocks. *Journal of Financial Economics* 9 (March): 3-18.

Basu, S. 1977. The Investment Performance of Common Stock in Relation to their Price/Earnings Ratios: A Test of the Efficient Market Hypothesis. *Journal of Finance* 32 (June): 663-682.

Basu, S. 1983. The relationship between earnings yields, market value and returns for NYSE common stocks: Further evidence. *Journal of Financial Economics* 12 (June): 19-46.

Black, F., M.C. Jensen, and M. Scholes. 1972. The Capital Asset Pricing Model: Some Empirical Tests. In *Studies in the Theory of Capital Markets,* ed. M.C. Jensen. New York: Praeger Publishers.

Black, F. and M. Scholes. 1973. The Pricing of Options and Corporate Liabilities. *Journal of Political Economy* 81 (May/June): 637-54.

Black, F. 1973. Yes Virginia, There is Hope: Tests of the Value Line Ranking System. *Financial Analysts Journal* 29 (September/October): 10-14.

Boland, J.C. 1980. Stock market seers? Investment managers are usually wrong at turning points. *Barrons* (September 1): 11-14.

Boquist, J.A., G.A. Racette, and G.G. Schlarbaum. 1975. Duration and Risk Assessment for Bonds and Common Stocks. *Journal of Finance* 30 (December): 1360-65.

Casabona, P.A., F.J. Fabozzi, and J.C. Francis. 1984. How to Apply Duration to Equity Analysis. *Journal of Portfolio Management* 10 (Winter): 52-58.

Cox, J.C., S.A. Ross and M. Rubinstein. 1979. Option pricing: A simplified approach. *Journal of Financial Economics* 7 (September): 229-263.

DeBondt, W.F.M. and R. Thaler. 1985. Does the Stock Market Overreact? *Journal of Finance* 40 (July): 793-808.

Dreman, D. 1982. The myth of market timing. *Forbes* (January 4): 292-93.

Einhorn, H.J and R. Hogarth. 1978. Confidence in Judgment: Persistence in the Illusion of Validity. *Psychological Review* 85: 395-416.

Estep, P.W. 1987. Security Analysis and Stock Selection: Turning Financial Information into Return Forecasts. *Financial Analysts Journal* 43 (July/August): 34-43.

Fama, E.F. 1965. The Behavior of Stock Market Prices. *Journal of Business* 38 (January): 34-105.

Fama, E.F. 1970. Efficient Capital Markets: A Review of Theory and Empirical Work. *Journal of Finance* 25 (May): 383-417.

Fama, E.F. and M. Blume. 1966. Filter Rules and Stock Market Trading. *Journal of Business* 39, Special Supplement (January): 226-241.

Fama, E.F., L. Fischer, M. Jensen, and R. Roll. 1969. The Adjustment of Stock Prices to New Information. *International Economic Review* 10 (February): 1-21.

Fama, E.F. and K. French. 1987. Permanent and Temporary Components of Stock Prices. CRSP Working Paper #178 (February).

Fisher, L. and R.L. Weil. 1971. Coping with the Risk of Interest Rate Fluctuations: Returns to Bondholders from Naive and Optimal Strategies. *Journal of Business* 44 (October): 408-431.

Friend, I., F.E. Brown, E.S. Herman, and D. Vickers. 1962. *A Study of Mutual Funds.* Washington, DC: Government Printing Office.

Fuller, R.J. and J.L. Farrell, Jr. 1987. *Modern Investments and Security Analysis.* New York: McGraw-Hill.

Gilovich, T., R. Vallone, and A. Tversky. 1985. The hot hand in basketball: On the misperception of random sequences. *Cognitive Psychology* 17: 295-314.

Graham, B. 1973. *The Intelligent Investor.* New York: Harper and Row.

Gross, L. 1982. *The Art of Selling Intangibles: How to Make Your Million($) by Investing Other People's Money.* New York: New York Institute of Finance.

Haugen, R.A. and D.W. Wichern. 1974. The Elasticity of Financial Assets. *Journal of Finance* 29 (September): 1229-1240.

Hicks, John R. 1939. *Value and Capital.* Cambridge: Oxford University Press.

Hirsch, T. *The Stock Trader's Almanac.* The Hirsch Organization.

Hopewell, M. and G.G. Kaufman. 1973. Bond Price Volatility and Term to Maturity: A Generalized Respecification. *American Economic Review* 4 (September): 749-753.

Jacobs, B. and K. Levy. 1988. Calendar Anomalies. *Financial Analysts Journal*. Forthcoming.

Jacobs, B. and K. Levy. 1988. On the Value of 'Value'. *Financial Analysts Journal*. Forthcoming.

Jacobs, B. and K. Levy. 1988. Trading Anomalies. In *A Complete Guide to Securities Transactions: Controlling Costs and Enhancing Performance*, ed. W. Wagner. New York: John Wiley & Sons. Forthcoming.

Jacobs, B. and K. Levy. 1988. Disentangling Equity Return Regularities: New Insights and Investment Opportunities. *Financial Analysts Journal*. Forthcoming.

Jacobs, B. and K. Levy. 1987. Investment Management: Opportunities in Anomalies? *Pension World* 23 (February): 46-47.

Jaffe, J.A. 1974. Special Information and Insider Trading. *Journal of Business* 47 (July): 410-428.

Jensen, M. 1969. Risk, the Pricing of Capital Assets and the Evaluation of Investment Portfolios. *Journal of Business* 42 (April): 167-247.

Jones, C.P., R.S. Rendleman Jr., and H.A. Latane. 1985. Earnings Announcements: Pre and Post Responses. *Journal of Portfolio Management* 11 (Spring): 28-32.

Joy, O.M., R.H. Litzenberger, and R.W. McEnally. 1977. The adjustment of Stock Prices to Announcements of Unanticipated Changes in Quarterly Earnings. *Journal of Accounting Research* 15 (Autumn): 207-255.

Kahneman, D. and A. Tversky. 1973. On the psychology of prediction. *Psychological Review* 80: 251-273.

Keim, D.B. 1983. Size-related anomalies and stock market seasonality: Further empirical evidence. *Journal of Financial Economics* 12 (June): 13-32.

Keim, D.B. 1985. Dividend yield and stock returns: Implications of abnormal January returns. *Journal of Financial Economics* 14 (September): 473-489.

Keim, D.B. 1986. Dividend Yields, Size and the January Effect. *Journal of Portfolio Management* 12 (Winter): 54-60.

Keim, D.B. 1986. The CAPM and Equity Return Regularities. *Financial Analysts Journal* 42 (May/June): 19-34.

Keim, D.B. 1987. Daily Returns and Size-Related Premiums: One More Time. *Journal of Portfolio Management* 13 (Winter): 41-47.

Knecht, L.D. and M.L. McCowin. 1987. Valuing Convertible Securities. In *The CFA Candidate Readings II*, 163-79. Charlottesville: The Institute of Chartered Financial Analysts.

Lanstein, R. and W.F. Sharpe. 1978. Duration and Security Risk. *Journal of Financial and Quantitative Analysis* 13 (November): 653-668.

Leibowitz, M.L., E.H. Sorensen, R.D. Arnott, and H.N. Hanson. 1987. *A Total Differential Approach to Equity Duration*. New York: Salomon Brothers Inc.

Levy, R.A. 1967. Relative Strength as a Criterion for Investment Selection. *Journal of Finance* 22 (December): .

Litzenberger, R. and K. Ramaswamy. 1979. The Effect of Personal Taxes and Dividends on Capital Asset Prices: Theory and Empirical Evidence. *Journal of Financial Economics* 7 (June): 163-195.

Livingston, M. 1978. Duration and Risk Assessment for Bonds and Common Stocks: A Note. *Journal of Finance* 33 (March): 293-295.

Macauley, F.R. 1938. *Some Theoretical Problems Suggested by the Movement of Interest Rates, Bond Yields, and Stock Prices Since 1856*. New York: National Bureau of Economic Research.

Merton, R. 1987. A Simple Model of Capital Market Equilibrium with Incomplete Information. *Journal of Finance* 42 (July): 483-510.

Nicholson, S.F. 1960. Price-Earnings Ratios. *Financial Analysts Journal* 16 (July/August): 43-45.

Oppenheimer, H. and G.G. Schlarbaum. 1981. Investing with Ben Graham: An *Ex Ante* Test of the Efficient Market Hypothesis. *Journal of Finance and Quantitative Analysis* (September): 341-360.

Reinganum, M.R. 1981. Misspecification of capital asset pricing: Empirical anomalies based on earnings' yields and market values. *Journal of Financial Economics* 9 (March): 19-46.

Reinganum, M.R. 1983. The anomalous stock market behavior of small firms in January: Empirical tests for tax-loss selling effects. *Journal of Financial Economics* 12 (June): 89-104.

Roberts, H. 1959. Stock Market "Patterns" and Financial Analysis: Methodological Suggestions. *Journal of Finance* 14 (March): 1-10.

Roll, R. 1977. A critique of the asset pricing theory's tests, part 1: On past and potential testability of the theory. *Journal of Financial Economics* 4 (March): 129-176.

Roll, R. and S.A. Ross. 1980. An Empirical Investigation of the Arbitrage Pricing Theory. *Journal of Finance* 35 (December): 1073-1103.

Rosenberg, B. and A. Rudd. 1982. Factor Related and Specific Returns of Common Stocks. *Journal of Finance* 37 (May): 543-554.

Rosenberg, C.N., Jr. 1986. *Investing With the Best*. New York, New York: John Wiley & Sons.

Ross, S.A. 1976. The Arbitrage Theory of Capital Asset Pricing. *Journal of Economic Theory* 13 (December): 341-360.

Rozeff, M.S. and W.R. Kinney, Jr. 1976. Capital market seasonality: The case of stock returns. *Journal of Financial Economics* 3 (October): 379-402.

Sharpe, W.F. 1963. A Simplified Model for Portfolio Analysis. *Management Science* 9 (January): 277-293.

Sharpe, W.F. 1964. Capital Asset Prices: A Theory of Market Equilibrium Under Conditions of Risk. *Journal of Finance* 19 (September): 425-442.

Sharpe, W.F. 1966. Mutual Fund Performance. *Journal of Business* 39, Special Supplement (January): 119-138.

Sharpe, W.F. 1985. *Investments*. 3d ed. Englewood Cliffs, NJ: Prentice Hall.

Shefrin, H. and M. Statman. 1985. The Disposition to Sell Winners Too Early and Ride Losers Too Long: Theory and Evidence. *Journal of Finance* 40 (July): 777-792.

Shefrin, H. and M. Statman. 1987. A behavioral finance solution to the noise trading puzzle. Santa Clara University Working Paper.

Solt, M. and M. Statman. 1987. How useful is the sentiment index? Santa Clara University Working Paper.

Sorensen, E.H. and D. Williamson. 1985. Some Evidence on the Value of Dividend Discount Models. *Financial Analysts Journal* 41 (November/December): 60-70.

Sorensen, E.H. and S.B. Kriechman. 1987. *Valuation Factors: Introducing the E-Model*. New York: Salomon Brothers Inc.

Sprinkel, B.W. 1964. *Money and Stock Prices*. Homewood, IL: Richard D. Irwin.

Treynor, J. 1987. Market Efficiency and the Bean Jar Experiment. *Financial Analysts Journal* 43 (May/June): 50-53.

Tversky, A. and D. Kahneman. 1986. Rational Choice and the Framing of Decisions. *Journal of Business* 59 Special Supplement (October): S251-S287.

Weiner, N. 1948. *Cybernetics or the Science of Communication and Control Process in Animals and Machines*. Cambridge, MA: MIT Press.

Self-Evaluation Examination Questions

1. Which of the following conditions is consistent with market efficiency:
   - I. No transaction costs.
   - II. All available information is costlessly available to all market participants.
   - III. All investors agree on the implications of current information for the distribution of future prices.
   - IV. Investor valuation errors are not independent.

   a) I.
   b) I and IV.
   c) II and III.
   d) I, II, and III.
   e) All of the above.

2. Research on the efficient market theory indicates that:
   a) The Capital Asset Pricing Model (CAPM) is an accurate asset pricing model.
   b) Investors are not able to outperform the market.
   c) The latest evidence on market efficiency is not consistent with earlier studies.
   d) All of the above.
   e) None of the above.

3. The most important part of an "engineered investment strategy" is a precise determination of how the strategy would have worked in the past.
   a) True.
   b) False.

4. According to Hagin, computer-based historical data frequently suffers from problems of:
   a) Inaccuracy.
   b) Omissions.
   c) Survivor bias.
   d) All of the above.
   e) None of the above.

5. According to Rosenberg, market cycles:
   a) May be illusions.
   b) May arise out of wishful thinking.
   c) Are signs of an inefficient market.
   d) All of the above.
   e) None of the above.

6. Which market cycle is statistically significant according to Rosenberg:
   a) Market-sector cycle.
   b) Liquid-stock cycle.
   c) Marketing cycle.
   d) Election cycle.

7. According to Statman, investors use full-fee stockbrokers because they:
   a) Provide more services to the investor.
   b) Play the role of scapegoat.
   c) Are able to give advice on a wide range of investment instruments.
   d) All of the above.

8. According to Statman, the higher returns on stocks of companies with low reputations are compensation for regret.

   a) True.
   b) False.

9. Recent empirical evidence is consistent with the efficient market hypothesis.

   a) True.
   b) False.

10. Jacobs and Levy describe several categories of anomalies, including:

    I.   Value-based regularities.
    II. Price-based regularities.
    III. Earnings expectations-based regularities.
    IV. Calendar-based regularities.

    a) I and II.
    b) I, II, and III.
    c) I, II, and IV.
    d) All of the above.

11. Jacobs and Levy's results show that which of the following effects exists in the naive form, but not in the pure form:

    a) The P/E effect.
    b) The small size effect.
    c) The neglect effect.
    d) The residual reversal effect.
    e) The cash flow/price effect.

12. According to Jacobs and Levy, which anomaly is a true pocket of market inefficiency:

    a) The P/E effect.
    b) The small size effect.
    c) The neglect effect.
    d) The residual reversal effect.
    e) The cash flow/price effect.

13. According to their results, Jacobs and Levy conclude that there is a clear linkage between pure returns to low P/E and returns to the overall stock market.

    a) True.
    b) False.

14. In comparison with an actively-managed portfolio, the typical index fund has:

    a) More stocks.
    b) No cash reserves.
    c) Detailed and constant monitoring.
    d) All of the above.
    e) None of the above.

15. According to Skelton, program trading techniques may be used to implement strategies other than management of an index fund.

    a) True.
    b) False.

16. According to Fogler, the function of security analysis is:
    a) To make financial forecasts.
    b) To generate DDM projections.
    c) To try to skew return distributions in your favor.
    d) To be knowledgeable about security characteristics.

17. Which of the following are potential problems with DDMs, according to Fogler:
    a) DDMs are sensitive to the time horizon.
    b) DDMs are sensitive to rates of return.
    c) DDMs do not provide explicit diversification.
    d) All of the above.
    e) None of the above.

18. Estep uses the following inputs in his T-model:
    a) Analysts' forecasts of return and economic growth statistics.
    b) Data on whether corporate management is good, whether products are proprietary, and whether the company faces foreign competition.
    c) Growth of equity, cashflow yield, and valuation change.
    d) Growth of equity, cashflow yield, and profit margin.

19. Estep is able to explain the relationship between rising ROE stocks and return using the T-model.
    a) True.
    b) False.

20. Stocks with long durations are characterized by:
    a) Low growth potential, stable earnings patterns, and low earnings sensitivity to changes in either real interest rates or inflation.
    b) High growth potential, stable earnings patterns, and low earnings sensitivity to changes in either real interest rates or inflation.
    c) High growth potential, variable earnings patterns, and low earnings sensitivity to changes in either real interest rates or inflation.
    d) Low growth potential, variable earnings patterns, and high earnings sensitivity to changes in either real interest rates or inflation.

21. According to Sorensen, in the 1980s long duration stocks experienced relatively high returns during periods of major falls in interest rates.
    a) True.
    b) False.

22. According to Aron, when Japanese earnings are adjusted to conform to U.S. accounting standards the P/E ratio drops to less than the U.S. P/E ratio.
    a) True.
    b) False.

23. According to Aron, Japanese accounting differs from U.S. GAAP on all of the following issues except:
    a) Tax Deductions
    b) Calculation of earnings per share.
    c) Consolidation of subsidiaries.
    d) Accounting for revenue.

24. In the individual era of investment, which of the following was true according to LeBaron:
    a) Pricing was important.
    b) Good news was a value component.
    c) Data sources were readily available.
    d) Stock prices were not affected by supply and demand.

25. According to LeBaron, which of the following eras are we now entering:
    a) The Institutional era of investment.
    b) The Individual era of investment.
    c) The Pension Fund era of investment.
    d) The Corporate era of investment.

26. According to Wagner, program trading is not an expensive way to trade.
    a) True.
    b) False.

27. Program traders help to ensure that an efficient pricing mechanism exists.
    a) True.
    b) False.

28. It is possible for convertibles to outperform the S&P 500, with somewhat less volatility.
    a) True.
    b) False.

29. The essence of the Harris approach to valuing convertible securities, as outlined by McCowin, is:
    a) To treat each convertible as a combination of a stock and a bond.
    b) To treat each convertible as a combination of a stock and a warrant.
    c) To treat each convertible as a combination of a bond and a warrant.
    d) None of the above.

30. The theoretical value of a convertible security is affected by:
    a) Changes in the value of the underlying equity security.
    b) Changes in interest rates.
    c) Changes in the premium.
    d) All of the above.

Self-Evaluation Examination Answers

See Schlarbaum:
1. d
2. c

See Hagin:
3. a
4. d

See Rosenberg:
5. d All of the above.
6. b The other phenomenon can be explained.

See Statman:
7. b
8. a True.

See Jacobs and Levy:
9. b False.
10. d
11. e
12. d
13. b Jacobs and Levy's results indicate the opposite.

See Skelton:
14. d All of the above.
15. a True.

See Fogler:
16. c
17. d All of the above.

See Estep:
18. c
19. b False. For some reason people overprice rising ROE stocks, which can not be explained using the T-model.

See Sorensen:
20. b
21. a True.

See Aron:
22. b False. The Japanese P/E is less than the U.S. P/E after adjusting for both differences in accounting and different capitalization rates.
23. d Aron never discusses accounting for revenue.

See LeBaron:
24. b
25. d

See Wagner:

26. b False.
27. b False.

See McCowin:

28. a True. See Table 1 of McCowin's presentation.
29. c
30. d